Passion To Profit

Knox

Preface

Turning your passion into a thriving business isn't just a fantasy; it's an attainable goal that anyone can reach with the right approach and tools. This book is crafted for dreamers, innovators, and anyone at any stage of life looking to convert their passions into profitable ventures. The journey to financial independence starts with leveraging what you love most and morphing that into a sustainable and rewarding business.

Within these pages, you'll find more than just success stories or financial advice. This guide is a comprehensive toolkit that offers practical strategies, insightful tips, and thought-provoking exercises designed to foster your entrepreneurial spirit and sharpen your business acumen. We will explore essential financial skills, innovative business models, and the importance of a growth mindset in achieving lasting success.

Whether you're a creative looking to monetize your art, a tech enthusiast aiming to launch a start-up, or someone exploring side hustles, this book is your mentor. It will challenge you to look beyond the ordinary, encourage you to embrace risks intelligently, and equip you with the knowledge to build and sustain a business that reflects your passions and values.

Introduction

The concept of achieving financial success might seem daunting or far-fetched, especially for those just embarking on their professional or creative journeys. However, the secret to financial empowerment doesn't necessarily lie in advanced degrees or decades of experience; it begins with the skills, interests, and passions you already possess.

This book demystifies the process of turning hobbies into income and provides a roadmap for navigating the complex world of personal finance and entrepreneurship. It breaks down the barriers of where to start and what to do next, offering clear, actionable steps for anyone, regardless of age or background.

From the outset, you'll learn how to identify profitable niches within your hobbies, understand the basics of setting up a business, and grasp the fundamentals of effective financial management. Each chapter is tailored to help you build on your existing talents, uncover opportunities for growth, and avoid common pitfalls that new entrepreneurs often encounter.

Moreover, this guide emphasizes the importance of adapting to economic changes, leveraging emerging technologies, and understanding market dynamics to stay competitive. With a blend of inspirational stories and practical advice, the book aims to ignite your entrepreneurial spirit and provide the tools needed to forge a path toward financial independence and personal fulfillment.

Table of Contents

Chapter 1: Discover Your Passion

"The key to making money is figuring out what you love and turning it into something valuable."

Turning a hobby or passion into a source of income is no longer an idea limited to just certain groups or professionals. Whether you're still in school, just starting out in the workforce, or even deep into your career, it's never too late—or too early—to harness your passions and transform them into profitable ventures. The key to success lies in discovering what truly excites you and exploring how to make it valuable to others.

This chapter is all about identifying what drives you. Once you know what that is, the possibilities for turning it into an income-generating activity are endless. Whether your passion lies in the arts, technology, sports, or a more specialized niche, there's room for you to share it with the world and get rewarded for doing so.

What Is a Passion, and Why Does It Matter?

A passion is more than just a pastime or hobby—it's something that energizes you, something you would gladly spend hours doing without feeling like it's "work." It could be a creative activity, a talent you have, or even a skill you've developed over time. When your passion becomes the core of what you do, you'll find that work no longer feels like a chore, but a part of who you are.

In a world that values authenticity and creativity, turning a passion into profit isn't just about making money—it's about building a life that's aligned with what you enjoy. Doing what you love helps you master it over time, opening up countless opportunities. The earlier or more often you tap into this passion, the more time you have to refine it and build a foundation for long-term success.

How to Identify Your Passion

For some people, identifying a passion comes naturally—they know what they love and what excites them. For others, it takes a bit more self-reflection. No matter where you fall on this spectrum, here are some ways to help uncover what you're truly passionate about:

1. **What Makes You Lose Track of Time?**
   - Think about the activities that make time fly by. Whether it's creating something, learning a new skill, or helping others in some way, the things that naturally absorb your attention are often connected to your passion.
2. **What Excites You?**
   - What gets you excited or motivated to take action? Consider the moments when you feel most energized, whether it's when you're creating, solving problems,

or building something new. These moments can offer clues to what you're truly passionate about.

3. **What Are You Naturally Good At?**
    o Sometimes, your passion aligns with a natural skill or talent you already possess. What have people complimented you on? What do you do effortlessly that others struggle with? Your natural abilities can often point to areas where you can find success.

4. **What Do You Talk About the Most?**
    o If you find yourself constantly talking about a particular topic, whether it's an activity, an industry, or a hobby, this could be an indicator of where your passion lies. Passionate conversations often reveal what truly matters to you.

5. **Explore New Activities and Skills:**
    o If you're still unsure, try exploring new hobbies, skills, or activities. You might find that your passion is something you haven't even discovered yet. The more you explore, the better chance you'll have of finding something that truly resonates with you.

Examples of Passion Turned into Profit

Passions come in many forms, and people have found ways to turn them into profit through a variety of creative approaches. Here are a few generalized examples to inspire you:

- **Sharing Knowledge and Expertise:**
  - If you're naturally good at something, whether it's teaching, writing, or solving problems, there's a demand for that knowledge. Many have successfully built businesses or online platforms by sharing their expertise with a wider audience through content, products, or services.
- **Creating and Selling Products:**
  - If you enjoy making things, from digital designs to physical crafts, there are numerous ways to sell what you create. Some have turned their passion for crafting, design, or art into income by selling their products directly to customers.
- **Providing Services:**
  - Many people are passionate about helping others, whether through tutoring, consulting, or offering specialized skills like web development or graphic design. This can be turned into a service-based business where your skills are exchanged for payment.

Finding Your Niche: The Key to Standing Out

Identifying your passion is just the first step. To truly succeed, you'll need to narrow it down into a specific niche. A niche is simply a focused area where your passion meets the needs or desires of others. It helps you stand out from the crowd by allowing you to target a specific audience who values what you offer.

For example, if you're passionate about fitness, your niche might be designing workout plans for beginners or helping people achieve fitness goals with limited equipment. If you love art, you might specialize in a particular style, such as portraiture or digital illustration. Finding your niche helps you sharpen your focus and develop your skills in a way that attracts people who are interested in what you offer.

Turning Your Passion into Profit: How to Get Started

Now that you've identified your passion and chosen your niche, it's time to start thinking about how you can turn it into a profitable venture. Here are some practical steps to help you get started:

1. **Research the Market:**
   - Who are the people that would be interested in your passion? Whether they're potential customers, clients, or an audience for your content, understanding who you're targeting is key. Study others who are already succeeding in similar areas, and see how they've built their audience or customer base.
2. **Start Sharing Your Work:**
   - No matter what your passion is, start by sharing it. Whether through social platforms, local events, or other mediums, getting your work out there is essential. This helps you gain feedback,

build an audience, and develop a presence in your chosen niche.

3. **Offer Your Services or Products:**
   o Once you've gained some visibility, you can start offering what you've created. Whether it's a service, a product, or content, begin to test how people respond to it. Remember, starting small is okay—the key is to gain experience and begin the journey.

4. **Refine Your Skills:**
   o As you begin to turn your passion into profit, focus on continually refining your skills. Keep learning and improving, and always look for ways to add value to the people you serve.

Exercises: Turning Passion into Action

Here are a few exercises to help you take the first steps toward discovering and monetizing your passion:

1. **Create a Passion List:**
   o Write down a list of everything you enjoy doing, no matter how small or trivial it seems. Once you've made your list, pick the top three activities that excite you the most.

2. **Identify a Niche:**
   o For each of your top three passions, think about how you can specialize. What specific need can you fulfill, or how can you make your passion stand

out? Write down a few ideas on how to narrow your focus.

3. **Research Opportunities:**
   - o For your top passion, research how others have turned similar interests into income. Look at how they've built an audience or customer base and the platforms they use to share or sell their work.

4. **Make a Plan:**
   - o Based on what you've learned, write out three simple steps you can take this week to start moving toward monetizing your passion. These steps could include creating a profile, sharing your work online, or reaching out to others in your niche.

Conclusion: Taking the First Step

Discovering your passion and turning it into something profitable doesn't happen overnight, but it starts with a single step: identifying what excites you. From there, the journey to monetizing your passion begins. In the next chapter, we'll dive into how the internet can be a powerful tool for turning your passion into profit by connecting you with a global audience.

Chapter 2: The Power of the Internet: Your Global Marketplace

---

"The internet isn't just a tool—it's a global stage where your passion can reach and impact people anywhere in the world."

Once you've identified your passion and started thinking about how to turn it into a profitable venture, the next step is leveraging the vast power of the internet. The online world has transformed the way we connect, share, and do business. Whether you're offering a service, selling a product, or creating content, the internet gives you access to a global audience, eliminating the limitations of location.

In this chapter, you'll learn how to build an online presence that effectively showcases your passion, how to grow an audience, and the steps you can take to start monetizing what you love.

Your Online Presence: Building the Foundation

Your online presence is the foundation of your success in today's world. It's where people will find you, learn about you, and decide whether to engage with your work. Your online presence can take many forms, depending on what you're offering. Whether it's through social profiles, a personal website, or an online shop, your presence must be a clear reflection of your passion and what you offer.

Here are a few essential elements to consider as you build your presence online:

1. **Clarity of Purpose**:
   o Be clear about what you do and who you're serving. Your online profile or website should immediately communicate what value you provide—whether it's a product, service, or information. A well-defined message helps attract the right audience.
2. **Consistency Across Platforms**:
   o If you're using multiple online platforms, ensure that your message, branding, and tone remain consistent. This creates a unified identity, making it easier for your audience to recognize and connect with you.
3. **Authenticity**:
   o People connect with real, authentic stories. Don't feel the need to present a perfect version of yourself online. Share your journey, your progress, and even your challenges. Authenticity builds trust, and trust is key to growing an audience.
4. **Value Before Monetization**:
   o Before jumping into monetization, focus on providing value to your audience. Whether it's helpful information, engaging content, or high-quality products, offering value first ensures that when you do introduce paid services or

products, your audience will already see the worth in supporting you.

Choosing the Right Platform for Your Passion

The internet offers a wide range of platforms, each suited to different types of content and services. Whether you're selling handmade products, creating educational content, or offering freelance services, choosing the right platform is essential.

Here are some general types of platforms to consider:

1. **Content Platforms**:
   - These are ideal for creators who want to share knowledge, showcase talents, or build a following through written, audio, or video content. People use content platforms to educate, entertain, or inspire others. These platforms are great for reaching a wide audience, building a community, and even creating subscription-based models for regular content.
2. **Marketplace Platforms**:
   - If you create physical or digital products, marketplace platforms allow you to sell your items to a global audience. These platforms typically handle the technical aspects of selling, such as payment processing and inventory management,

giving you more time to focus on your craft.

3. **Service-Based Platforms**:
   - For those offering freelance or consulting services, service-based platforms connect you with clients seeking specialized skills. Whether it's graphic design, tutoring, writing, or coding, service platforms provide a marketplace where clients can hire you for specific projects or ongoing work.

Each of these platforms has unique features, so the key is to match the platform to the type of work you do and where your audience is most likely to engage.

Building Your Audience: Growing from Zero

One of the most challenging aspects of starting online is building your audience from scratch. However, with consistency and the right strategies, you can steadily grow a community that is engaged with and excited about your work. Remember, building an audience takes time, but the effort you put in today will pay off in the long run.

Here's how to get started:

1. **Post Regularly**:
   - Whether you're sharing content, offering updates, or posting about new products, consistency is critical. Posting regularly

helps keep you in front of your audience, and most platforms favor content creators who are active. Plan a schedule that works for you and stick to it.

2. **Engage With Your Followers**:
   - Engagement is a two-way street. When someone comments, likes, or shares your content, take the time to respond or acknowledge them. Building a loyal audience requires more than just posting—you need to foster connections with the people who support you.

3. **Create Valuable Content**:
   - People follow creators, brands, and businesses that add value to their lives. Whether that value is educational, entertaining, or practical, focus on creating content that benefits your audience. This keeps people coming back for more and encourages them to share your work with others.

4. **Collaborate and Network**:
   - Collaborating with others in your field or niche is a powerful way to grow. When you collaborate, you expose your work to a new audience, while also providing value to someone else's followers. Look for mutually beneficial opportunities to work with others, whether through shared projects, guest appearances, or shout-outs.

Turning Your Audience into Supporters

Once you've started building an audience, the next step is figuring out how to turn that audience into active supporters. This doesn't necessarily mean immediately asking people to buy something from you—it's about creating ways for your audience to support your work while continuing to receive value in return.

Here are a few ways to start monetizing your online presence:

1. **Sponsored Content and Partnerships**:
   - When you've built a sizable audience, you may have the opportunity to partner with brands or companies that align with your message or passion. Partnerships allow you to feature products or services while earning a commission or fee. It's important to only promote things that align with your values and what your audience expects from you.
2. **Selling Products**:
   - If you're offering a product, whether digital or physical, you can begin selling directly to your audience once you've built a following. The key is to create products that resonate with the needs and interests of your audience. These could be anything from artwork and designs to educational guides or personalized services.
3. **Memberships and Subscription Models**:
   - Some platforms allow creators to offer premium content in exchange for a membership or subscription fee. This

could be in the form of exclusive behind-the-scenes content, early access to new products or videos, or special tutorials that go deeper into your expertise.

4. **Affiliate Marketing**:
   - Affiliate marketing is another option where you promote products or services from other companies and earn a commission when your audience makes a purchase through your unique link. It's important to only recommend products that you personally believe in and that align with your brand.

Exercise: Building Your Online Foundation

Here's a set of actions to help you lay the groundwork for a strong online presence and start growing your audience:

1. **Choose Your Primary Platform**:
   - Based on your passion and the content or product you want to share, select the platform that best suits your goals. Write down why you chose this platform and what you plan to achieve with it.
2. **Set Up a Profile or Storefront**:
   - Create your profile or online store. Be sure to choose a username or store name that reflects your passion and is easy to remember. Write a short bio or description that clearly communicates

what you do and why people should follow or support you.

3. **Plan Your First Post or Product Launch**:

    o   Take the first step by sharing your passion with your audience. Whether it's a blog post, video, artwork, or product listing, put something out into the world that represents your work. Don't wait for it to be perfect—starting is more important than being flawless.

Conclusion: The Global Stage is Yours

The internet provides endless opportunities to share your passion with the world and connect with people who will appreciate and support your work. By establishing a clear and authentic online presence, choosing the right platform, and consistently engaging with your audience, you'll be well on your way to turning your passion into a profitable venture.

In the next chapter, we'll explore how to take your newfound online presence and transform it into a structured business or project. Whether you're freelancing, building a side hustle, or starting a full-time venture, having a plan in place is key to long-term success.

Chapter 3: Setting Up Your First Venture—Turning Passion into Action

"An idea is only the beginning—action is what turns it into reality."

You've discovered your passion, and you've learned how to use the internet to share it with the world. Now, it's time to take the next big step: turning your passion into a structured venture. Whether you're looking to start a business, offer a service, or simply organize your efforts, creating a clear plan will help you navigate the path toward success.

This chapter will walk you through setting up your first venture, providing practical steps to turn your passion into something that can generate consistent income. Don't worry if this seems daunting—it's not about creating a large corporation overnight. It's about starting small, testing your ideas, and gradually building something that can grow over time.

The Power of Planning: Why You Need a Clear Vision

Before you dive into the nuts and bolts of setting up a venture, the first step is developing a clear vision. This doesn't need to be a complex business plan, but having clarity about what you want to achieve will provide direction and keep you focused.

Ask yourself the following questions:

1. **What is my goal?**
   - Are you looking to build a long-term business, or are you exploring a side project for extra income? Clarifying your goal helps you determine how much time and effort to invest.
2. **Who is my audience?**
   - Understanding your audience or customer base is critical. Who benefits from your product, service, or content? Knowing who you're targeting will help you tailor your message, design your products, or shape your services to meet their needs.
3. **What problem am I solving?**
   - Whether you're offering art, advice, or a specific product, think about the value you're providing. What problem or need does your passion address? People support ventures that offer something useful, whether it's entertainment, education, or a solution to a problem they face.

Once you've answered these questions, you'll have a clearer idea of where you want to take your venture and how to make it relevant to the people who will support it.

Step 1: Organizing Your Ideas and Efforts

The first step to turning your passion into action is to organize your ideas. When you're passionate about something, it's easy to be flooded with ideas about what you want to do. However, the key to success is focusing on manageable, concrete steps that can move you forward.

Here's how you can organize your efforts:

1. **Break Your Big Idea into Small Steps**:
    - Instead of trying to do everything at once, break down your big idea into smaller, actionable steps. For example, if your goal is to sell handmade products online, your steps could include designing your first product, researching the best platform to sell on, and setting up a profile or store.
2. **Set Realistic Goals**:
    - Setting specific, achievable goals will keep you motivated and prevent overwhelm. Instead of vague goals like "grow my business," set clear targets like "get my first five customers" or "post one new piece of content each week." These smaller goals are easier to measure and help you stay on track.
3. **Keep Track of Your Progress**:
    - Use a simple tool like a notebook, a digital document, or an app to track your progress. Celebrate your small wins along the way, and adjust your plan as needed. Staying organized will help you

manage your time and energy more effectively.

Step 2: Creating a Simple Business or Project Plan

Even if you're starting small, having a basic plan for your venture is essential. This plan will serve as your roadmap, guiding you through the initial stages and helping you focus on the important tasks at hand.

Here are the core elements of a simple plan:

1. **Define Your Product or Service**:
   - Be clear about what you're offering, whether it's a product, service, or content. Make sure it aligns with your passion and fills a need for your audience.
2. **Understand Your Audience**:
   - Dig deeper into your target audience. Who are they? Where do they spend their time online? What motivates them? This understanding will shape your marketing efforts and help you connect more effectively with potential supporters.
3. **Decide on Pricing**:
   - If you're selling a product or service, research what similar offerings cost and set a fair price for your work. Don't undersell yourself, but also be mindful of what your audience is willing to pay.

> Over time, as you build experience and credibility, you can adjust your pricing.

4. **Choose a Platform**:
   - Decide where you will conduct your business or share your project. This could be an online platform for selling products, a website for booking services, or a content-sharing site. Choose the platform that best suits your audience and goals.
5. **Budget and Resources**:
   - If your venture requires startup costs, such as materials or tools, make sure you plan your budget. Keep track of expenses, and start small so you can scale up over time. You don't need a large investment to get started—many successful ventures begin with minimal resources.

Step 3: Taking Action—Launch and Learn

Once you have a plan in place, it's time to take action. This stage is where many people hesitate, often because they want everything to be perfect. But the truth is, the best way to learn is by doing. Don't wait for perfection—start with what you have and improve as you go.

Here's how to launch and learn:

1. **Start Small**:
   - Don't feel pressured to have everything figured out. Start with one product, one

service, or one piece of content, and gradually build from there. Small, consistent actions add up over time.

2. **Seek Feedback**:
    o   Feedback is crucial for growth. Ask your audience, customers, or clients for honest opinions on your work. Use their feedback to make improvements and refine what you offer.

3. **Learn from Mistakes**:
    o   Mistakes are part of the process. Instead of seeing them as setbacks, view them as opportunities to learn. Whether it's pricing adjustments, improving your product, or changing how you market your work, every mistake brings you closer to success.

4. **Celebrate Progress**:
    o   Every step forward is worth celebrating. Whether it's your first sale, your first client, or your first 100 followers, recognize the effort you've put in and reward yourself for reaching new milestones.

Step 4: Building Long-Term Success

Turning your passion into a venture is exciting, but it's also a long-term journey. As you begin to see results, it's important to maintain momentum and keep growing. Here's how you can continue building on your success:

1. **Keep Innovating**:

- o Don't be afraid to try new things. Whether it's experimenting with new ideas, launching new products, or finding different ways to engage with your audience, innovation keeps your venture fresh and exciting.

2. **Build Relationships**:
   - o Your audience, customers, and collaborators are key to your long-term success. Build strong relationships with the people who support your work, and stay connected with them through consistent communication and engagement.

3. **Stay Adaptable**:
   - o The world is constantly changing, and so is the online marketplace. Be open to adapting your approach based on trends, feedback, or new opportunities that arise. Flexibility is key to staying relevant and successful.

4. **Set New Goals**:
   - o Once you've achieved your initial goals, set new ones that challenge you to grow further. This could mean expanding your product line, growing your audience, or increasing your income. Setting new goals keeps you motivated and forward-thinking.

Exercise: Your First Steps Toward Launch

Let's put what you've learned into action! Here are a few exercises to help you launch your venture:

1. **Define Your First Offering**:
    o   Write down what your first product, service, or piece of content will be. Be specific about what you're offering and how it benefits your audience.
2. **Set a Goal**:
    o   What is your first measurable goal? It could be gaining your first five customers, reaching 100 followers, or completing a specific project. Set a goal that feels challenging but achievable.
3. **Take the First Action**:
    o   Write down one small action you can take today to move your venture forward. Whether it's creating a profile, sharing your work, or reaching out to potential customers, taking that first step is crucial.

Conclusion: You've Got This—Now Go Create

Starting your first venture might feel like a leap, but remember that every successful business or project started with a single step. By organizing your ideas, creating a plan, and taking action, you're already ahead of the curve. The more you learn, adapt, and improve, the closer you'll get to turning your passion into a sustainable source of income or fulfillment.

In the next chapter, we'll explore how to manage your time, resources, and efforts to maintain balance while growing your venture. Success doesn't happen overnight, but with dedication and smart management, you can steadily build the future you envision.

Chapter 4: Managing Your Time, Resources, and Efforts

"The key to success isn't just hard work—it's smart management of your time, resources, and energy."

You've set up your first venture, and you're taking the necessary steps to turn your passion into something real. But the road to success isn't just about putting in long hours or pouring all your resources into your project. To build something sustainable, you need to learn how to manage your time, resources, and efforts effectively.

In this chapter, we'll explore strategies for staying productive without burning out, managing your resources wisely, and keeping your venture running smoothly even as it grows. Success is about working smart, not just working hard.

The Balance Between Passion and Discipline

Passion is what gets you started, but discipline is what keeps you going. Many people dive into their ventures with immense enthusiasm, working long hours fuelled by passion. But what happens when the initial excitement fades or when things don't go according to plan? That's where discipline comes in.

The difference between those who succeed and those who give up often comes down to consistency. Here are some ways to strike a balance between passion and discipline:

1. **Set a Daily Routine:**
   - Passion gives you energy, but routines give you stability. Establish a daily or weekly routine for working on your venture, even if it's just an hour or two per day. Over time, these small, consistent efforts will compound into significant results.
2. **Prioritize What Matters Most:**
   - You may have endless ideas and tasks swirling around in your mind, but not all tasks are equally important. Learn to prioritize by asking yourself, "What will move the needle the most for my venture?" Whether it's refining your product, connecting with customers, or improving your skills, focus on what delivers the greatest impact.
3. **Celebrate Small Wins:**
   - Discipline isn't about working non-stop; it's about finding a sustainable pace. Along the way, celebrate small victories. These could be finishing a project, landing a new client, or even just making significant progress. Recognizing these moments will keep you motivated and provide fuel for the long journey ahead.
4. **Have an Accountability Partner:**
   - Sometimes, staying disciplined is easier when you have someone to keep you accountable. Find a partner, mentor, or

friend who can check in with you regularly and keep you on track. They can also provide encouragement and help you overcome challenges.

Time Management: The Key to Productivity

Time management is not just about squeezing in as much work as possible into each day—it's about working efficiently and effectively. Here are strategies that can help you get more done without feeling overwhelmed:

1. **Time Blocking:**
   - Time blocking is one of the most effective ways to manage your time. This method involves breaking your day into chunks of time dedicated to specific tasks. Instead of juggling multiple tasks at once, you focus on one task during each time block, which improves productivity and reduces distractions.

   Example: If you dedicate two hours in the morning to product development and one hour in the afternoon to marketing, you ensure that you make progress in both areas without feeling scattered.

2. **Batching Similar Tasks:**
   - Group similar tasks together to maximize efficiency. For instance, if you're creating content, dedicate a few hours to writing all your blog posts or

recording multiple videos instead of spreading them out over several days. This reduces the mental strain of constantly switching between different tasks.

Example: If you spend an entire morning planning and creating social media posts for the week, you'll have more time to focus on other aspects of your venture in the days that follow.

3. **The 80/20 Rule (Pareto Principle):**
   - The Pareto Principle suggests that 80% of your results come from 20% of your efforts. Focus on the tasks that deliver the highest impact. Instead of trying to do everything, concentrate on the activities that generate the most significant returns.

Example: If creating content is driving most of your traffic or sales, prioritize content creation and reduce time spent on tasks that aren't yielding much value.

4. **Delegating and Outsourcing:**
   - As your venture grows, you may find that some tasks are taking up too much of your time, but they're not your core strengths. Learn to delegate or outsource tasks that don't require your direct attention, such as administrative work or certain technical tasks. This frees up your time to focus on what you do best.

Resource Management: Working Smarter, Not Harder

When starting out, it's essential to make the most of the resources you have. Whether it's money, tools, or even skills, resource management can make the difference between success and failure. Here's how to approach it:

1. **Start with What You Have:**
   - o Many people feel they need a significant budget or expensive equipment to start their venture. However, you can often begin with what you already have and upgrade as your venture grows. It's more important to start and gain experience than to wait for the "perfect" setup.

   Example: If you're starting a freelance design business, you don't need the most advanced software or tools right away. Use free or low-cost alternatives to create your first projects and reinvest your earnings into better tools as you grow.

2. **Track Every Expense:**
   - o Whether you're investing in tools, materials, or advertising, it's essential to track your spending carefully. Use a spreadsheet or an app to record every expense, no matter how small. This will give you a clear picture of where your money is going and allow you to make smarter decisions about future investments.

Example: If you notice that a certain type of marketing is costing more than it's bringing in, you can adjust your strategy and focus on more cost-effective methods.

3. **Learn to Be Resourceful:**
   - Being resourceful means finding creative solutions to challenges, especially when you have limited resources. This could involve bartering skills, using free tools and platforms, or partnering with others to achieve common goals.

Example: If you're an artist but can't afford a photographer, consider trading services with a photographer who needs artwork for their portfolio. This way, both parties benefit without spending money.

4. **Reinvest in Growth:**
   - As your venture begins to generate income, reinvest a portion of that money into growing your business. This could mean upgrading your equipment, purchasing better materials, or investing in education to improve your skills. Reinvesting wisely ensures that your venture continues to grow and evolve.

Example: If your online store starts making regular sales, consider reinvesting some of the profits into advertising or improving your packaging to enhance customer satisfaction.

Energy Management: Staying Healthy and Focused

Success requires energy—not just physical energy but mental and emotional energy as well. To keep your venture moving forward, it's essential to manage your energy levels and avoid burnout. Here's how to stay energized and focused:

1. **Take Breaks Regularly:**
   - Working non-stop may seem productive in the short term, but it leads to exhaustion and burnout. Take regular breaks to recharge your mind and body. Even stepping away for a few minutes can help you return to your work with renewed focus and creativity.

   Example: Use the Pomodoro technique, where you work for 25 minutes and then take a 5-minute break. After four cycles, take a longer break. This method helps maintain focus while preventing burnout.

2. **Get Enough Sleep:**
   - Sleep is one of the most important factors for maintaining your energy and productivity. A well-rested mind is more focused, creative, and able to handle challenges. Prioritize getting enough sleep, even if you feel tempted to work late into the night.

   Example: Create a consistent sleep schedule, and aim for 7-8 hours of sleep per night. Avoid screens and stimulating activities an hour before bed to help you wind down and sleep better.

3. **Stay Physically Active:**
   - Physical activity boosts your energy levels, improves your mood, and enhances mental clarity. Even short bursts of exercise can help you stay focused and energized throughout the day.

   Example: If you're sitting at a desk for long periods, take short walks, stretch, or do light exercises during your breaks to keep your body moving and your mind sharp.

4. **Practice Mindfulness and Relaxation:**
   - Mental energy is just as important as physical energy. Practice mindfulness, meditation, or relaxation techniques to reduce stress and maintain a positive mindset. Taking care of your mental health is key to staying resilient in the face of challenges.

   Example: Spend 10-15 minutes each day practicing mindfulness or deep breathing exercises. This can help you clear your mind, reduce anxiety, and approach your work with a calm, focused attitude.

Exercise: Putting It All into Practice

Let's apply what you've learned to your venture. These exercises will help you manage your time, resources, and energy more effectively:

1. **Create a Weekly Time Block Schedule**:
   - Plan your week using time blocks. Identify your most important tasks and assign specific time slots for each. Include time for breaks, personal activities, and other responsibilities.
2. **Track Your Spending and Investments**:
   - Create a simple financial tracker where you record all expenses related to your venture. Review it at the end of each month to evaluate whether you're spending wisely and what adjustments you can make.
3. **Identify Energy Drains**:
   - Take note of activities or habits that drain your energy—whether it's working too long without breaks, skipping meals, or spending too much time on non-essential tasks. Once you've identified these drains, make a plan to reduce or eliminate them.

   Example: If you find that spending too much time on social media is draining your energy, set limits for how much time you spend online, or schedule specific times of day for checking updates so that it doesn't interfere with your productivity.

3. **Set Reinvestment Goals**:

- o As your venture starts to grow and generate income, plan how much of your earnings you'll reinvest into improving your business. This could include upgrading your equipment, buying better materials, or investing in education to enhance your skills.

Example: Set a goal to reinvest a percentage of your profits back into your venture. If you earn $100, decide that you'll put 10-20% of that back into resources or tools that will help your business grow.

Conclusion: Sustainable Success Through Smart Management

Building a successful venture requires more than just passion and talent—it demands thoughtful management of your time, resources, and energy. By learning to prioritize, delegate, and pace yourself, you can avoid burnout while making steady progress toward your goals. Remember, success is a marathon, not a sprint.

As you move forward, always keep in mind that smart management isn't about doing everything at once. It's about focusing on what matters most, using your resources wisely, and ensuring that you have the energy to keep going.

In the next chapter, we'll dive into the importance of building relationships and networking. Whether you're looking for collaborators, customers, or mentors, the right connections can take your venture to new heights.

Chapter 5: Building Relationships and Networking—The Power of Connections

"No venture succeeds in isolation—your network is your net worth."

While talent and hard work are essential, no one achieves success entirely on their own. Whether you're starting a business, offering a service, or sharing your passion, the relationships you build can make a significant difference in how far you go. Building a strong network opens doors to opportunities, partnerships, customers, and mentors who can guide you on your journey.

In this chapter, we'll explore how to create meaningful connections, expand your network, and leverage relationships to grow your venture. We'll also discuss the importance of building trust and reciprocity within your network. After all, relationships are the foundation of every successful Endeavor.

Why Relationships Matter in Your Venture

In today's interconnected world, relationships can be more valuable than any tool or resource. Whether you're working with others in your industry, collaborating with fellow creators, or building a loyal customer base, relationships create the support system you need to thrive. Here's why they matter:

1. **Access to Knowledge and Experience**:
   - When you connect with others, you gain access to their knowledge and experience. They may have insights into your industry, ideas on how to solve specific problems, or tips on growing your venture more effectively.

2. **Opportunities for Collaboration**:
   - Collaborating with others can lead to projects or ventures that would have been impossible to achieve on your own. Whether it's a joint project, a shared marketing effort, or cross-promotion, working with others allows you to reach new audiences and expand your influence.

3. **Support and Encouragement**:
   - The road to success is full of challenges, and having a supportive network can help you stay motivated. When you build meaningful relationships, you have people who believe in your mission and offer support when things get tough.

4. **Expanding Your Reach**:
   - Word-of-mouth is one of the most powerful tools for growing your venture. When people in your network trust and support you, they're more likely to recommend you to others, whether through social media, professional connections, or personal recommendations.

Building Trust and Authentic Connections

When building relationships, the goal isn't to network for the sake of gaining something—it's to create meaningful, authentic connections. These are relationships based on mutual respect, shared interests, and a genuine desire to support each other's growth.

Here are some principles to keep in mind when building authentic relationships:

1. **Be Genuinely Interested in Others**:
   - The most successful relationships are built on mutual interest. When you approach someone, take the time to learn about their work, interests, and goals. Show genuine curiosity and appreciation for what they do, and find ways to connect over shared passions or experiences.
2. **Give Before You Receive**:
   - Don't approach networking with the mindset of "What can I get from this person?" Instead, focus on how you can provide value to others. Whether it's offering advice, sharing a helpful resource, or providing feedback, giving first builds trust and shows that you care about more than just your own success.
3. **Be Authentic**:
   - People can tell when you're being insincere. Authenticity goes a long way in building strong, lasting relationships. Be yourself, and don't try to force

connections. The best relationships grow naturally over time when both parties have mutual respect and shared goals.

4. **Consistency Matters**:
    o Building relationships takes time, and consistency is key. Stay in touch with people in your network, check in on their progress, and offer support when needed. A simple message of encouragement or congratulations can strengthen your relationships over time.

How to Build and Expand Your Network

Networking doesn't have to be intimidating. In fact, with the right mindset, it can be enjoyable and incredibly rewarding. Here are strategies to help you build and expand your network effectively:

1. **Start with Your Existing Connections**:
    o Look at the relationships you already have. This could be friends, family members, classmates, colleagues, or people you've interacted with through your work. Reach out to them, share what you're working on, and see if there are opportunities to collaborate or support each other.
2. **Join Communities Related to Your Passion**:
    o Whether online or offline, communities offer a great way to meet people who share your interests. Look for groups, forums, or organizations where people gather around a common passion or

industry. Participating in discussions, attending events, and contributing value helps you build relationships within these communities.

3. **Attend Industry Events**:
   - If there are local or virtual events related to your field, make an effort to attend. Conferences, workshops, and networking events are excellent opportunities to meet others, learn from experts, and share your work with a wider audience.

4. **Leverage social media and Online Platforms**:
   - Social media can be a powerful tool for building relationships, especially if you're working in a creative field. By following and engaging with people whose work you admire, you can start building connections. Don't be afraid to reach out through a message or comment—sometimes, a simple introduction is all it takes to spark a new relationship.

5. **Offer Help and Collaboration**:
   - Don't wait for others to approach you. If you see someone working on a project or initiative that aligns with your skills or passion, offer your help. Collaborating on projects can lead to long-term partnerships and deeper connections.

Nurturing Your Network: The Importance of Reciprocity

Building a strong network doesn't stop at making connections—it requires continuous nurturing and reciprocity. People are more likely to support you when they feel supported in return. Here's how to maintain a healthy, mutually beneficial network:

1. **Check In Regularly**:
    - Don't let months go by without connecting with people in your network. Send a quick message, ask how their project is going, or comment on their latest work. Small gestures of interest go a long way in keeping relationships strong.
2. **Share Opportunities**:
    - If you come across an opportunity that could benefit someone in your network—whether it's a job posting, a speaking engagement, or a new client—share it with them. By providing value and helping others succeed, you create a sense of reciprocity.
3. **Celebrate Their Success**:
    - When someone in your network achieves a milestone or reaches a goal, be sure to celebrate with them. Acknowledging and supporting their success strengthens your relationship and shows that you genuinely care about their growth.
4. **Collaborate Often**:

- o Collaboration deepens relationships. Look for ways to partner with people in your network on projects, whether it's a joint event, a shared venture, or simply cross-promoting each other's work. By working together, you build trust and amplify each other's efforts.

Building Long-Term Mentorships

One of the most valuable relationships you can develop in your network is a mentorship. A mentor is someone with more experience who can offer guidance, advice, and support as you grow your venture. Here's how to find and build a mentor relationship:

1. **Identify Potential Mentors**:
   - o Look for people who have achieved success in your field or have the experience you admire. This could be someone you've met at an event, someone you've connected with online, or even a leader in your industry whose work you follow.
2. **Approach with Respect**:
   - o When reaching out to potential mentors, approach with respect and humility. Don't immediately ask them to be your mentor. Instead, express your admiration for their work, ask thoughtful questions, and seek advice on a specific challenge or goal you're working on.
3. **Be Open to Learning**:

- o A good mentorship is built on a willingness to learn and grow. Be open to feedback and advice, and don't be afraid to ask questions. Show your mentor that you're serious about improving and making progress.

4. **Give Back to Your Mentor**:
   - o While your mentor is there to help you, mentorship is a two-way relationship. Find ways to give back, whether it's by sharing your own insights, offering assistance with a project, or simply expressing gratitude. Mentorship is a long-term relationship built on mutual respect and support.

Exercise: Expanding and Strengthening Your Network

Let's put what you've learned into action. Here are a few exercises to help you build and strengthen your network:

1. **Make a List of Current Connections**:
   - o Identify 5-10 people you're already connected with who might be valuable to your venture. Reach out to them with a message of encouragement, an update on your work, or an offer to collaborate.
2. **Join a New Community**:
   - o Find an online group, forum, or local organization related to your field or passion. Join the group and introduce

yourself. Start engaging by offering value, whether it's by answering questions, sharing resources, or participating in discussions.

3. **Reach Out to a Potential Mentor**:
   o Identify someone you admire and respect in your field. Send a thoughtful message or email expressing your admiration and asking for advice on a specific issue. Be respectful and open to learning from their experience.

4. **Collaborate on a Project**:
   o Think of one person in your network who you could collaborate with. Whether it's a joint content piece, a project, or a cross-promotion, reach out to them with an offer to work together and create something of value.

Conclusion: Strength in Numbers

Your network is one of your most valuable assets. The relationships you build today can lead to opportunities, support, and collaboration that will take your venture to the next level. But remember, networking isn't about what you can gain—it's about building meaningful, lasting connections based on trust, mutual respect, and shared success. The stronger your relationships, the more support and opportunities you'll have along the way.

In the next chapter, we'll dive into understanding your audience and how to market your passion effectively. Whether you're selling a product, offering a service, or creating content, understanding your audience is the key to turning your venture into a lasting success.

Chapter 6: Understanding Your Audience and Marketing Your Passion

"It's not just about what you create—it's about who you're creating it for."

You've worked hard to turn your passion into a venture, but no matter how great your product, service, or content is, success hinges on one thing: connecting with the right audience. Understanding who your audience is, what they care about, and how to communicate with them is crucial for growing your venture. This chapter will guide you through identifying your target audience and creating a marketing strategy that speaks directly to them.

Why Understanding Your Audience is Key?

No venture succeeds without an audience. Whether you're selling a product, providing a service, or sharing content, your audience is the foundation of your success. Understanding your audience allows you to create products or services that truly meet their needs, craft messages that resonate with them, and build relationships that lead to loyalty and growth.

Here are a few reasons why knowing your audience is vital:

1. **Tailoring Your Offerings:**

- o When you understand your audience, you can design your offerings to solve their specific problems, meet their desires, or fulfill their needs. This makes your venture more valuable to them.

2. **Effective Communication**:
   - o Knowing who your audience is allows you to speak their language. You'll be able to craft messages that appeal to their interests, values, and emotions, making it easier to connect with them.

3. **Building Loyalty**:
   - o When your audience feels understood and valued, they're more likely to become loyal supporters. Loyalty leads to repeat business, referrals, and long-term success.

4. **Guiding Your Marketing Strategy**:
   - o Your marketing efforts will be much more effective when you know where your audience spends time, what content they consume, and what motivates them to take action. This saves you time, money, and effort by focusing on what works.

Step 1: Identifying Your Target Audience

The first step to understanding your audience is to identify exactly who they are. Your target audience is the group of people who are most likely to be interested in what you offer. These are the people who will benefit the most from your products, services, or content.

Here's how to define your target audience:

1. **Demographics**:
   - Start with basic demographic information like age, gender, location, income level, and education. Are you targeting teenagers, young professionals, or retirees? Do they live in urban or rural areas? Are they budget-conscious, or are they willing to spend more on quality products?
2. **Interests and Hobbies**:
   - What are the hobbies, interests, and activities your audience enjoys? If you're offering a fitness-related service, your audience is likely interested in health, exercise, and wellness. If you're selling handmade goods, they might appreciate creativity and craftsmanship.
3. **Problems and Pain Points**:
   - Identify the problems your audience faces and how your venture can solve them. For example, if you're providing educational content, your audience might be struggling to understand a specific subject or skill. Your offering should address these pain points directly.
4. **Values and Motivations**:
   - What does your audience value? Do they care about sustainability, quality, or convenience? What motivates them to make purchasing decisions? Understanding their values and motivations helps you create messages that resonate deeply with them.
5. **Behaviour**:

- o Where does your audience spend time online? Do they prefer reading blogs, watching videos, or scrolling through social media? Understanding their online behavior helps you know where to reach them and how to communicate effectively.

Step 2: Crafting Your Marketing Message

Once you know who your audience is, the next step is to create a marketing message that speaks directly to them. Your marketing message is the way you communicate the value of your venture to your audience. It should explain what you offer, why it matters to them, and why they should choose you over competitors.

Here's how to craft a compelling marketing message:

1. **Focus on Benefits, Not Features**:
   - o When describing your offering, focus on how it benefits your audience, not just what it does. For example, if you're selling a time management app, don't just describe its features—talk about how it will save users time, reduce stress, and help them be more productive.

   Example: Instead of saying, "Our app tracks your time," say, "Our app helps you take control of your day and get more done with less stress."

2. **Speak Their Language**:
   - Use language that your audience understands and connects with. Avoid technical jargon or overly complex explanations unless your audience is highly specialized. The goal is to make your message clear, relatable, and easy to understand.

Example: If your audience is new to fitness, avoid using complicated workout terminology. Instead, use simple, friendly language that encourages them to get started.

3. **Address Their Pain Points**:
   - Show that you understand the challenges your audience faces and how your offering can solve those problems. When your audience feels that you understand their struggles, they're more likely to trust and engage with you.

Example: If you're offering career coaching, you could say, "Are you feeling stuck in your career? We help you gain the confidence and skills you need to take the next step and land your dream job."

4. **Highlight What Makes You Unique**:
   - What sets you apart from the competition? Highlight the unique aspects of your venture that make it stand out. This could be your personal story, the quality of your product, or a specialized approach that others don't offer.

Example: "Our handmade products aren't just beautiful—they're crafted with eco-friendly materials, so you can feel good about your purchase."

Step 3: Choosing the Right Marketing Channels

Now that you've crafted your message, it's time to decide where and how to deliver it. Choosing the right marketing channels means understanding where your audience spends their time and which platforms they trust. Not every platform will be right for your venture, so it's important to focus on the ones that align with your audience's behaviour.

Here are some common marketing channels and when to use them:

1. **Social Media**:
   - Social media platforms are ideal for reaching a wide audience, sharing content, and building community. Choose platforms that align with your audience's interests and habits. Visual platforms are great for artists and designers, while more text-heavy platforms may suit writers and educators.

   Example: If your audience is young and enjoys visual content, social media could be the best way to engage them with eye-catching images, videos, or tutorials.

2. **Email Marketing**:
   o Email marketing is a direct and effective way to communicate with your audience. Building an email list allows you to keep your audience informed about new offerings, special promotions, or upcoming events. The key to success in email marketing is providing value in every message.

Example: If you're offering a service like coaching, email marketing allows you to nurture leads, share success stories, and offer helpful tips that keep your audience engaged over time.

3. **Content Marketing (Blogs, Videos, Articles)**:
   o Content marketing is a great way to build authority and trust with your audience. By sharing valuable information, tips, or insights related to your niche, you position yourself as an expert while helping your audience solve problems.

Example: If you're a graphic designer, writing blog posts about design trends, offering tutorials, or creating videos that show your process can attract clients who are interested in your services.

4. **Paid Advertising**:
   o If you have a budget, paid advertising can help you reach a wider audience

quickly. Whether through social media ads, search engine marketing, or display ads, paid campaigns allow you to target specific demographics and drive traffic to your website or storefront.

Example: If you're launching a new product, a well-placed paid ad can help you attract your target audience quickly, especially if you're still building your organic reach.

5. **Collaborations and Partnerships**:
    o   Collaborating with other creators, businesses, or influencers in your niche can be an effective way to grow your audience. Cross-promoting each other's work introduces you to new potential customers or followers while building valuable relationships.

    Example: If you're offering a fitness program, collaborating with a nutrition expert to create joint content can introduce both of you to new audiences who are interested in a holistic approach to wellness.

Step 4: Engaging and Building Loyalty with Your Audience

Once you've attracted your audience, the next step is to engage them and build loyalty. Loyal customers or followers are more likely to support you in the long term, spread the word about your venture, and become advocates for your brand.

Here's how to engage your audience and foster loyalty:

1. **Provide Consistent Value**:
   - Consistency is key to keeping your audience engaged. Whether through content, updates, or product releases, make sure you're consistently offering value. This could be in the form of helpful tips, inspiring stories, or exclusive deals for loyal customers.
2. **Engage in Two-Way Communication**:
   - Don't just talk at your audience—talk with them. Respond to comments, answer questions, and show appreciation for their support. Building a dialogue creates a sense of community and makes your audience feel valued.
3. **Offer Personalization**:
   - Whenever possible, offer personalized experiences to your audience. This could be through customized products, tailored advice, or personal thank-you messages to customers. Personalization makes your audience feel seen and appreciated.
4. **Incentivize Loyalty**:
   - Reward your most loyal customers or followers with exclusive offers, early access to products, or special content. Offering incentives for repeat business or loyalty programs can keep your audience coming back and make them feel valued for their support.

Example: If you run an online store, consider offering a discount or free shipping to customers who make repeat purchases. If you create content, give your loyal followers early access to new videos or blog posts.

5. **Share Your Story**:
   - o People connect with stories. Share your journey—how you started, the challenges you've faced, and the victories you've achieved. Being transparent and authentic makes your audience feel like they're part of your journey, which strengthens their connection to your brand.

Step 5: Measuring Your Success

It's essential to track the effectiveness of your marketing efforts. Measuring your success helps you understand what's working, what needs improvement, and how you can optimize your approach. Here are a few key metrics to track, depending on your marketing channels:

1. **Website Traffic**:
   - o If you have a website, use analytics tools to track how many visitors you're getting, where they're coming from, and which pages they're spending the most time on. This can help you see which marketing channels are driving the most traffic and what content resonates with your audience.
2. **Engagement**:

- o On social media or content platforms, track engagement metrics like likes, comments, shares, and views. High engagement shows that your audience is actively interacting with your content, which is a good indicator of interest and loyalty.

3. **Conversion Rate**:
   - o Conversion rate refers to the percentage of people who take a desired action, such as making a purchase, signing up for your newsletter, or filling out a contact form. Improving your conversion rate means making it easier for your audience to take action on what you offer.

4. **Email Open and Click Rates**:
   - o If you're using email marketing, track how many people open your emails and click on the links inside. Low open or click rates may indicate that your subject lines or content need improvement, while high rates show that your audience is interested in what you're sharing.

5. **Customer Feedback and Reviews**:
   - o Listen to what your customers are saying through reviews, testimonials, and direct feedback. Positive feedback can help attract new customers, while negative feedback gives you valuable insights into what needs to be improved.

6. **Return on Investment (ROI)**:
   - o If you're spending money on marketing, track your ROI to make sure your investments are paying off. Compare the revenue you've generated from your marketing efforts to the amount you've

spent on advertising, tools, or campaigns.

Exercise: Understanding and Engaging Your Audience

Now that you have a better understanding of how to identify and engage your audience, here are some exercises to put this knowledge into action:

1. **Create an Audience Persona**:
   - Write down a detailed description of your ideal customer or audience member. Include demographics, interests, values, and behaviors. What challenges do they face, and how does your product or service solve them?
2. **Craft a Marketing Message**:
   - Using the principles discussed in this chapter, write a compelling marketing message that speaks directly to your audience's needs and desires. Focus on the benefits your venture provides and what makes you unique.
3. **Choose Two Marketing Channels**:
   - Identify two marketing channels where your audience spends the most time. Make a plan for how you'll engage them on those platforms, whether through social media posts, emails, blog content, or paid ads.
4. **Track Engagement for a Week**:

- o Monitor your engagement metrics on social media or your website for a week. Track likes, comments, shares, or any increase in website traffic. Analyze what type of content or message gets the most engagement.

Conclusion: Creating Lasting Connections with Your Audience

Understanding your audience is one of the most important aspects of running a successful venture. When you know who your audience is, how to communicate with them, and where to find them, you can create stronger connections, deliver more value, and ultimately grow your business or project. Your audience is the heart of your success, and by focusing on building trust, loyalty, and engagement, you'll create a community that supports and champions your work.

In the next chapter, we'll dive deeper into the financial aspects of your venture, covering everything from budgeting to reinvestment strategies that ensure your venture grows sustainably.

Chapter 7: Managing Your Finances—Budgeting and Growing Your Venture

"A successful venture isn't just built on passion—it's built on smart financial management."

Whether you're just starting out or you've been running your venture for a while, managing your finances is critical to its long-term success. Proper budgeting, smart investments, and efficient use of resources allow you to grow sustainably without running into financial trouble. In this chapter, we'll explore how to create a solid budget for your venture, handle income and expenses, and plan for future growth through smart reinvestment.

Why Financial Management Matters

Managing your finances properly is essential for several reasons:

1. **Staying in Control**:
   o Without a clear understanding of your income and expenses, it's easy to overspend, fall into debt, or lose track of your financial goals. Financial management helps you stay in control and make informed decisions.
2. **Sustainable Growth**:

- o By carefully managing your finances, you can reinvest in your venture at the right times and in the right areas. This ensures sustainable growth without overextending yourself or risking financial stability.

3. **Planning for the Future**:
   - o Smart financial planning allows you to set aside money for future opportunities, whether that's expanding your venture, investing in new tools, or saving for unexpected expenses.

4. **Profitability**:
   - o At the end of the day, your venture needs to be profitable to survive. Good financial management ensures that your revenue exceeds your costs, allowing you to turn your passion into a financially viable business.

Step 1: Creating a Budget for Your Venture

The foundation of financial management is a solid budget. A budget helps you keep track of your income and expenses, and ensures that you're using your resources wisely. Here's how to create a simple, effective budget for your venture:

1. **List All Your Expenses**:
   - o Start by listing all the expenses required to run your venture. These could include materials, equipment, tools, marketing costs, subscriptions, and any other

necessary expenses. Be thorough—small costs can add up over time.

Example: If you're running an online store, your expenses might include the cost of materials, packaging, shipping, website hosting, and advertising.

2. **Track Your Income**:
   o Record all the income you're generating from your venture, whether it's from sales, services, or other sources. Make sure to separate one-time income from recurring income so you can plan accordingly.

Example: If you're offering freelance services, track the income from each project or client. If you sell products, track the income from each sale, including any fees you may need to account for.

3. **Calculate Profit Margin**:
   o Your profit margin is the amount of money you're making after subtracting your expenses from your income. This gives you a clear picture of how much money you're keeping after covering costs.

Example: If you generate $1,000 in income and have $700 in expenses, your profit margin is 30%. This tells you how efficiently you're running your venture and whether you need to adjust your pricing or expenses to improve profitability.

1. **Set Financial Goals**:
    - Based on your budget, set financial goals for the next month, quarter, or year. These goals could include increasing revenue, reducing costs, or reaching a specific profit margin. Having clear financial goals helps you stay focused and measure progress.

    Example: If your profit margin is 30%, you might set a goal to increase it to 40% over the next six months by finding ways to reduce expenses or increasing your pricing.

Step 2: Tracking and Managing Cash Flow

Cash flow refers to the movement of money into and out of your venture. Positive cash flow means you're bringing in more money than you're spending, while negative cash flow means the opposite. Managing your cash flow is crucial to ensuring that your venture has enough money to cover expenses, reinvest, and grow.

Here's how to manage your cash flow effectively:

1. **Monitor Cash Flow Regularly**:
    - Keep a close eye on your cash flow by reviewing your income and expenses regularly. Use a simple spreadsheet or financial management tool to track how much money is coming in and going out each month. This helps you spot potential issues before they become problems.

2. **Separate Personal and Business Finances**:
    - o If possible, keep your personal and business finances separate. This makes it easier to track your venture's financial health and prevents confusion when managing income and expenses.

    Example: Open a separate bank account for your venture. This allows you to easily monitor business transactions without mixing them with personal expenses.

3. **Plan for Seasonal or Irregular Income**:
    - o Many ventures experience fluctuations in income throughout the year. If your income is seasonal or irregular, plan for the slow periods by setting aside money during the high-income months. This ensures you have enough cash flow to cover expenses even during leaner times.

    Example: If you know your venture earns more revenue in the holiday season, make sure to save a portion of that income to cover expenses during the slower months.

4. **Negotiate Payment Terms**:
    - o If you're working with clients or suppliers, try to negotiate favorable payment terms that improve your cash flow. For example, request shorter payment terms from clients (such as payment within 14 days) to ensure you receive income faster, while negotiating longer payment terms with suppliers if possible.

Step 3: Reinvesting in Your Venture for Growth

As your venture starts generating income, it's important to reinvest a portion of that money back into the business. Reinvestment helps you grow, improve your products or services, and stay competitive.

Here are smart ways to reinvest in your venture:

1. **Upgrade Tools and Equipment**:
    - Investing in better tools, software, or equipment can improve the quality of your work and increase efficiency. As your venture grows, upgrading your resources allows you to deliver better results and take on more projects or customers.

    Example: If you're a photographer, reinvesting in a higher-quality camera or editing software can help you produce more professional work and attract higher-paying clients.

2. **Expand Marketing Efforts**:
    - Reinvesting in marketing can help you reach a larger audience and generate more sales or leads. Whether through social media advertising, email campaigns, or collaborations, spending money on marketing can result in long-term growth.

Example: If your venture is generating consistent sales, reinvest in paid ads to reach new customers or build brand awareness.

3. **Improve Product or Service Offerings**:
   o Reinvestment can also mean improving your products or services. This could include enhancing features, adding new offerings, or increasing the quality of materials. These improvements make your venture more appealing and help retain customers.

Example: If you're selling handmade products, reinvest in higher-quality materials or offer customization options to increase the value of your products.

4. **Invest in Your Own Learning**:
   o Sometimes, the best investment you can make is in yourself. Taking courses, attending workshops, or learning new skills can directly benefit your venture. The more knowledge and expertise you gain, the better equipped you'll be to grow and succeed.

Example: If you're running a business online, investing in a course on digital marketing or e-commerce strategies can help you improve your sales and customer reach.

Step 4: Planning for the Future

As your venture grows, it's important to think long-term. Having a financial plan for the future ensures that you're prepared for growth opportunities, market changes, or unexpected challenges. Here's how to plan for the future of your venture:

1. **Build a Financial Cushion**:
   - Set aside a portion of your income to create a financial cushion, or emergency fund, for your venture. This fund can help you weather unexpected expenses, market downturns, or slow periods without putting your business at risk.

   Example: Aim to save three to six months' worth of expenses in your emergency fund. This ensures that your venture remains stable even if income temporarily decreases.

2. **Explore New Revenue Streams**:
   - As your venture grows, consider adding new revenue streams to diversify your income. This could mean offering additional products, services, or even creating passive income opportunities through digital products or affiliate marketing.

   Example: If you're a graphic designer, you could create digital design templates to sell alongside your custom services, creating a new source of income without significantly increasing your workload.

3. **Plan for Scaling**:
   o Scaling your venture means expanding it to reach more customers or offer more services. As you plan for growth, consider how you'll manage increased demand, additional expenses, and the need for more resources.

   Example: If your venture grows to the point where you can't handle everything yourself, you might plan to hire an assistant or outsource certain tasks, such as bookkeeping or customer service.

Exercise: Getting a Grip on Your Finances

Now it's time to put these financial strategies into action. Here are some exercises to help you manage your finances more effectively:

1. **Create a Monthly Budget**:
   o List all your venture's expenses and income sources, and create a simple budget for the month. Track how much you spend and earn, and adjust your budget as needed to improve your profit margin.
2. **Analyse Your Cash Flow**:
   o Review your cash flow for the past three months. Identify any patterns, such as periods of high or low income, and evaluate whether your cash flow is positive or negative. Based on your analysis, make adjustments to improve

your cash flow, such as cutting unnecessary expenses or finding ways to boost income during slow periods.

3. **Set Reinvestment Goals**:
   - Determine how much of your monthly or quarterly income you'll reinvest in your venture. Set clear goals for where you want to reinvest, whether it's upgrading tools, expanding your marketing, or improving your product or service offerings.

4. **Build an Emergency Fund**:
   - Start building a financial cushion by setting aside a percentage of your monthly profits. Your goal should be to create an emergency fund that covers at least three to six months of your operating expenses.

5. **Explore a New Revenue Stream**:
   - Identify one potential new revenue stream that aligns with your venture. This could be a new product, service, or passive income opportunity. Plan how you will introduce this new offering and track its impact on your overall income.

Conclusion: The Foundation of Financial Success

Smart financial management is the backbone of a successful venture. By creating a budget, managing cash flow, reinvesting strategically, and planning for the future, you ensure that your venture not only survives but thrives. Remember, success isn't just about how much you earn—it's about how well you manage what you have and how you plan for growth.

In the next chapter, we'll explore the importance of continuous learning and adapting to change, ensuring that your venture stays relevant and competitive in a fast-evolving world.

Chapter 8: Continuous Learning and Adapting to Change

"Success in any venture requires a willingness to learn, grow, and adapt in an ever-changing world."

The business world and market landscapes are constantly evolving. New technologies, trends, customer preferences, and competitive pressures emerge regularly, making adaptability a key skill for anyone running a venture. The most successful entrepreneurs and creators aren't just the ones who start with great ideas—they're the ones who continuously learn, adapt, and evolve as the world changes around them.

In this chapter, we'll explore how to maintain a mindset of lifelong learning, how to embrace change, and the importance of staying flexible in the face of challenges. Adapting to change and staying open to new knowledge will not only keep your venture relevant but also set you apart in a competitive marketplace.

Why Continuous Learning Matters

The journey to success doesn't end once you've launched your venture—it's a continuous process of growth and adaptation. Here's why a mindset of continuous learning is essential:

1. **Staying Competitive**:
   - Industries evolve, and new competitors will always emerge. The more you learn and stay updated with trends, tools, and customer preferences, the better equipped you'll be to maintain a competitive edge.
2. **Improving Your Skills**:
   - Mastery takes time and practice. Whether it's learning a new marketing strategy, improving your craft, or mastering a new technology, continuous learning helps you enhance the quality of your work and grow your venture.
3. **Identifying Opportunities**:
   - Learning allows you to spot new trends, technologies, or market gaps that you can take advantage of. By staying informed and adaptable, you'll be in a better position to pivot when new opportunities arise.
4. **Navigating Challenges**:
   - Every venture face challenges, whether it's a sudden market shift, a new competitor, or an internal roadblock. Continuous learning helps you develop problem-solving skills, giving you the tools to adapt and thrive in the face of adversity.

Step 1: Cultivating a Lifelong Learning Mindset

Learning doesn't stop after school—it's a lifelong process that helps you grow both personally and professionally. Cultivating a learning mindset means staying curious, being open to new ideas, and never settling for what you already know. Here's how to foster that mindset:

1. **Stay Curious**:
   - Approach everything with a sense of curiosity. Ask questions, explore new topics, and stay open to learning from everyone around you, whether they're peers, mentors, or customers. Curiosity drives innovation and helps you see things from different perspectives.
2. **Be Open to Feedback**:
   - Constructive feedback is one of the best ways to learn and improve. Be open to receiving feedback from customers, clients, colleagues, or mentors, and view it as an opportunity to grow. The most successful people are those who actively seek out ways to improve.
3. **Commit to Regular Learning**:
   - Make learning a regular part of your routine. This could be as simple as reading an article, watching a tutorial, or attending an online class. By committing to continuous education, you ensure that you're always growing and evolving.
4. **Challenge Yourself**:

- o Don't be afraid to step out of your comfort zone. Trying new things, learning unfamiliar skills, and taking on new challenges helps you grow faster and builds your resilience. It's through pushing your limits that you discover new strengths.

Step 2: Adapting to Change

Change is inevitable, but how you respond to it makes all the difference. Successful entrepreneurs and creators know how to pivot, when necessary, adjust their strategies, and embrace new directions. Here's how to adapt to change without losing focus:

1. **Embrace Flexibility**:
    - o Flexibility is the ability to shift gears when needed. Whether it's adjusting your business model, changing your product offerings, or rethinking your marketing strategy, being flexible allows you to stay relevant in a constantly shifting environment.

    Example: If your venture focuses on in-person services and an unexpected event (like a global pandemic) forces people to stay at home, you might need to adapt by offering online services or creating digital products.

2. **Keep an Eye on Trends**:
    - o Stay informed about industry trends and changes in consumer behavior. This

doesn't mean you have to chase every trend, but being aware of what's happening in your market can help you anticipate changes and adjust your approach before competitors do.

Example: If you're running an e-commerce business and notice a growing trend toward sustainable packaging, adopting eco-friendly practices early on can give you a competitive advantage and appeal to environmentally conscious customers.

3. **Don't Fear Failure—Learn from It**:
   - Failure is often seen as something to avoid, but it's one of the greatest learning tools available. Instead of fearing failure, embrace it as part of the learning process. Every mistake or setback is an opportunity to improve and grow stronger.

Example: If you launch a product that doesn't perform well, analyse what went wrong. Did you misjudge the market? Was the pricing off? Did the marketing message fail to resonate? Use this experience to make smarter decisions in the future.

4. **Pivot When Necessary**:
   - Sometimes, you may need to pivot—a significant change in direction for your venture. This could mean offering a different product, targeting a new audience, or shifting your business model entirely. Pivoting isn't a sign of

failure; it's a strategic response to change.

Example: If you've been focusing on selling a physical product but notice that demand for digital versions is growing, you might pivot by creating a downloadable version of your product or offering an online service.

Step 3: Learning New Skills to Stay Ahead

Continuous learning goes hand in hand with skill development. The world is changing rapidly, and acquiring new skills can give you a significant advantage in your field. Here's how to stay ahead through skill development:

1. **Identify Skills You Want to Learn**:
   - Start by identifying the skills that would benefit your venture the most. These could be technical skills, marketing skills, communication skills, or even management skills. Focus on areas that align with your goals and where you see growth opportunities.

   Example: If your goal is to grow your online presence, learning digital marketing, SEO (search engine optimization), or social media management might be beneficial skills to acquire.

2. **Find Learning Resources**:

o There are countless resources available to help you learn new skills. From online courses and workshops to free tutorials and books, the key is finding the right resource that fits your learning style and schedule.

Example: Platforms that offer a wide range of courses, podcasts, and blogs are great starting points for learning. Consider attending webinars, joining professional groups, or watching instructional videos in your field of interest.

3. **Practice Consistently**:
   o Learning new skills is one thing—applying them is another. Make time to practice what you've learned and integrate new skills into your daily work. Consistent practice leads to mastery.

Example: If you're learning a new software program or marketing tool, set aside time each week to practice using it. Create sample projects, run tests, or apply what you've learned in real-world scenarios.

4. **Stay Curious About Emerging Technologies**:
   o New technologies often create opportunities for growth and innovation. Stay curious about emerging technologies in your field, whether it's AI, automation tools, or new design software. Even if you don't adopt these technologies right away, staying

informed allows you to act quickly when needed.

Example: If you're in the design industry, staying up to date on the latest graphic design software or 3D modelling tools can open up new avenues for creative work and attract clients looking for cutting-edge services.

Step 4: Staying Resilient Through Challenges

Adapting to change and learning new skills requires resilience. Challenges and setbacks are inevitable, but resilience allows you to push through obstacles and keep moving forward. Here's how to build resilience as you navigate your journey:

1. **Develop a Growth Mindset**:
   - A growth mindset is the belief that skills and intelligence can be developed through effort, learning, and persistence. People with a growth mindset view challenges as opportunities to grow rather than as barriers to success. This mindset helps you stay motivated, even when things get tough.

   Example: If you encounter a challenging project or task, instead of feeling overwhelmed, approach it with the mindset that you can improve through practice and effort.

2. **Build a Support Network**:
    - o Surround yourself with people who support and believe in your goals. A strong network of friends, colleagues, and mentors can provide valuable advice, encouragement, and guidance when you're facing challenges or difficult decisions.

Example: Join professional groups or online communities in your field where you can share experiences, ask questions, and learn from others.

3. **Celebrate Small Wins**:
    - o Progress often happens in small steps, not giant leaps. Celebrate your small victories along the way, whether it's mastering a new skill, completing a project, or overcoming a challenge. Recognizing your progress keeps you motivated and reminds you of how far you've come.

Example: If you've successfully implemented a new marketing strategy, take a moment to acknowledge your accomplishment before moving on to the next goal.

4. **Focus on Long-Term Goals**:
    - o While it's important to adapt and make adjustments in the short term, always keep your long-term goals in mind. Stay focused on the bigger picture and remember why you started your venture in the first place. This perspective helps

you stay resilient when facing temporary setbacks.

Exercise: Adapting and Learning

Here are a few exercises to help you cultivate a mindset of continuous learning and adaptability:

1. **Identify a Skill to Learn**:
   - Choose one skill that would benefit your venture or help you grow personally. Research resources—books, online courses, tutorials—and create a plan to start learning that skill. Dedicate time each week to practice and improve.
2. **Analyse a Recent Challenge**:
   - Think about a recent challenge or setback you faced in your venture. Reflect on what went wrong, what you learned from the experience, and how you could approach it differently in the future. Use this reflection to develop strategies for adapting more effectively next time.
3. **Set Up a Learning Schedule**:
   - Set aside specific time each week for learning something new. This could be reading industry news, taking an online course, or attending a webinar. Commit to this learning time just like any other task in your business.
4. **Track Your Progress**:
   - Keep a journal or a log where you record what you're learning, how you're

applying new skills, and the progress you're making. Tracking your learning journey will help you see how far you've come and keep you motivated to continue growing.

Conclusion: The Journey of Continuous Learning

Success is not a destination; it's a journey of constant growth, learning, and adaptation. By embracing a mindset of lifelong learning and staying flexible in the face of change, you ensure that your venture continues to thrive no matter what challenges arise. Remember, the most successful entrepreneurs and creators aren't those who know everything—they're the ones who are always willing to learn something new.

In the next chapter, we'll explore how to maintain a healthy work-life balance, ensuring that you stay energized, productive, and fulfilled as you continue to grow your venture.

Chapter 9: Maintaining Work-Life Balance—Sustaining Your Passion and Well-Being

"Success doesn't mean burning out—true success is finding harmony between your work and your life."

Running a venture is exciting and fulfilling, but it can also be all-consuming. Whether you're balancing multiple responsibilities, growing a new business, or managing a side hustle, it's easy to become overwhelmed or exhausted. Finding a balance between your work and personal life is essential to maintaining your well-being, sustaining your passion, and ensuring long-term success.

In this chapter, we'll explore the importance of work-life balance and provide practical strategies for managing your time and energy. When you're able to create a healthy balance, you'll not only be more productive but also more fulfilled in both your work and personal life.

Why Work-Life Balance is Important

Maintaining a balance between work and personal life isn't just about feeling good—it's about sustaining your physical and mental health while keeping your passion alive. Here's why work-life balance matters:

1. **Preventing Burnout**:
   o Burnout occurs when you're overwhelmed by stress, working long hours without rest, and feeling emotionally drained. Burnout can cause a loss of motivation, productivity, and even physical health problems. A balanced work-life approach helps you avoid burnout and stay energized for the long run.
2. **Boosting Productivity**:
   o Taking time to rest and recharge actually makes you more productive. When you allow yourself regular breaks and time away from work, you return with renewed focus and creativity. A rested mind is more effective than a tired one.
3. **Maintaining Relationships**:
   o Your personal relationships, whether with family, friends, or partners, are vital to your overall well-being. Work-life balance ensures that you have time to nurture these relationships, which provide emotional support and happiness.
4. **Sustaining Passion**:
   o When you're overworked, it's easy to lose the passion and excitement that first drove you to start your venture. By creating balance, you protect your enthusiasm and keep your passion alive, ensuring that you continue to enjoy what you do.

Step 1: Setting Boundaries Between Work and Personal Life

The first step to achieving work-life balance is setting clear boundaries between your work and personal life. Without boundaries, it's easy for work to spill over into your personal time, leading to stress and exhaustion. Here's how to set and maintain boundaries:

1. **Designate Specific Work Hours**:
   - Set clear work hours and stick to them. Whether you're working on your venture full-time or part-time, having specific hours dedicated to work helps create structure and prevents work from taking over your entire day.

   Example: If you run your business from home, set specific hours when you focus on work (such as 9 AM to 5 PM) and avoid working outside of those hours unless absolutely necessary.

2. **Create a Separate Workspace**:
   - If possible, create a designated workspace that's separate from your personal spaces. This helps you mentally separate work from leisure, making it easier to "leave" work at the end of the day, even if you're working from home.

   Example: Set up a desk or corner of a room where you do all your work-related tasks. Avoid working from places associated with relaxation, like your bed or couch.

3. **Learn to Say No**:
   o Saying "no" to additional work or responsibilities when your plate is full is essential for maintaining balance. While it's tempting to take on more, overcommitting can lead to stress and burnout. Protect your time by only saying yes to opportunities that align with your goals and values.

   Example: If you're asked to take on a project that would cut into your personal time or overwhelm your schedule, politely decline or negotiate a timeline that works better for you.

4. **Turn Off Notifications**:
   o When you're done with work for the day, turn off work-related notifications on your phone or computer. Constant notifications can blur the lines between work and personal time, making it hard to fully disconnect and relax.

Step 2: Prioritizing Self-Care and Well-Being

Work-life balance is about more than just managing your time—it's also about taking care of your physical and mental well-being. Prioritizing self-care ensures that you stay healthy, energized, and focused on both your work and personal life. Here's how to incorporate self-care into your routine:

1. **Schedule Regular Breaks**:
   - Working for long periods without breaks can lead to mental fatigue and burnout. Schedule regular breaks throughout your day to step away from work, stretch, take a walk, or simply rest your mind.

   Example: Use the Pomodoro Technique, which involves working for 25 minutes and then taking a 5-minute break. After four work intervals, take a longer 15–30-minute break to recharge.

2. **Stay Physically Active**:
   - Regular physical activity boosts your energy levels, improves mood, and reduces stress. Incorporating exercise into your routine—even a short walk or a few minutes of stretching—can make a significant difference in your well-being.

   Example: Start your day with a 15-minute walk or a quick yoga session to energize yourself. If you have a sedentary job, schedule breaks for stretching or light exercise throughout the day.

3. **Get Enough Sleep**:
   - Sleep is essential for maintaining productivity and focus. When you're well-rested, you're more creative, resilient, and able to handle the demands of your venture. Prioritize getting 7-8 hours of sleep each night to ensure you're at your best.

   Example: Create a bedtime routine that helps you wind down and signals to your body that it's time to sleep. Avoid screens and stimulating activities at least an hour before bed to improve sleep quality.

4. **Practice Mindfulness and Stress Management**:
   o Managing stress is key to maintaining balance. Incorporate mindfulness practices such as meditation, deep breathing exercises, or journaling into your routine to reduce stress and stay grounded.

   Example: Spend 10 minutes each day practicing mindfulness or meditation. This simple practice can help you clear your mind, reduce anxiety, and improve focus.

Step 3: Managing Your Time Effectively

Effective time management is essential for balancing work and personal life. By managing your time well, you can maximize productivity during work hours and ensure that you have plenty of time left for rest, hobbies, and relationships. Here are some strategies for managing your time:

1. **Prioritize Your Tasks**:
   o Not every task is equally important. Focus on the tasks that have the highest impact on your venture and prioritize them over less critical tasks. This ensures that you're using your time

effectively and making progress on what matters most.

Example: At the start of each day, identify your top three priorities and focus on completing them before moving on to less important tasks. This helps you stay productive without getting overwhelmed.

2. **Use Time Blocks**:
   o Time blocking involves scheduling specific blocks of time for different tasks throughout the day. By dedicating focused time to each task, you reduce distractions and make the most of your work hours.

Example: Block out time in your calendar for different activities such as product development, marketing, and administrative work. During each time block, focus solely on that task to maximize efficiency.

3. **Delegate or Outsource**:
   o As your venture grows, you may find that certain tasks are taking up too much of your time. If possible, delegate or outsource tasks that don't require your direct attention, such as bookkeeping, customer service, or content creation.

Example: If you're spending too much time on accounting, consider hiring a freelance bookkeeper or using an accounting software that automates the process.

4. **Set Realistic Goals**:
   - It's important to set achievable goals for each day or week. Unrealistic goals lead to frustration and stress. Break larger projects into smaller, manageable tasks, and celebrate progress along the way.

Example: Instead of setting a goal to "launch a website" in one week, break it down into smaller tasks like "design homepage," "write content," and "test functionality." Completing each small task moves you closer to the overall goal.

Step 4: Making Time for What Matters Most

Work-life balance isn't just about managing your workload—it's about making time for the things that matter most to you outside of work. Whether it's spending time with family, pursuing hobbies, or simply relaxing, creating space for personal fulfillment is key to long-term happiness and success.

1. **Schedule Personal Time**:
   - Just as you schedule work tasks, schedule time for personal activities. Whether it's a weekly dinner with family, time for hobbies, or simply relaxing with a good book, blocking out time for these activities ensures they don't get overlooked.

Example: Set aside an hour each evening to disconnect from work and focus on personal interests, whether it's reading, playing an instrument, or enjoying time with loved ones.

2. **Unplug Regularly**:
   - In today's hyper-connected world, it's easy to feel like you're always "on." Make it a habit to unplug from work and technology regularly. Disconnecting helps you recharge and return to work with fresh energy and perspective.

   Example: Designate one day or evening each week where you unplug from work emails, social media, and notifications. Use this time to recharge and focus on your personal life.

3. **Pursue Hobbies and Passions**:
   - Don't forget to nurture your non-work-related hobbies and passions. Engaging in activities you love outside of work provides a sense of joy, creativity, and fulfillment that enhances your overall well-being. Pursuing hobbies can also be a great way to relieve stress and disconnect from the pressures of running your venture.

Example: If you enjoy painting, gardening, playing music, or cooking, schedule time each week to engage in those activities purely for enjoyment. This allows you to relax and recharge outside of work.

4. **Make Time for Relationships**:
   - Strong relationships provide emotional support, joy, and balance. Prioritize spending time with family, friends, and

loved ones, whether it's through shared activities, meals, or simple conversations. Nurturing relationships strengthens your personal life and gives you the resilience to handle challenges at work.

Example: Schedule regular family dinners, coffee catch-ups with friends, or weekend outings. These moments of connection help you recharge and maintain a healthy work-life balance.

Step 5: Recognizing When You're Out of Balance

Even with the best intentions, it's easy to lose track of work-life balance, especially during busy or stressful periods. Recognizing the signs of imbalance early allows you to make adjustments before burnout sets in. Here are a few signs that you might need to re-evaluate your balance:

1. **Constant Fatigue**:
    o If you're feeling tired all the time, even after resting, it may be a sign that you're overworking and not giving yourself enough downtime. Fatigue can affect your productivity, creativity, and overall well-being.
2. **Lack of Motivation**:
    o If your passion for your work has started to fade and you're finding it hard to stay

motivated, it might be due to burnout. This is often a sign that you need to take a step back and recharge.

3. **Neglecting Personal Relationships**:
   - When work takes up all your time and energy, personal relationships can suffer. If you notice you're spending less time with loved ones or missing out on important moments, it may be time to reassess your work schedule.

4. **Physical and Emotional Stress**:
   - Work-related stress can manifest physically (headaches, muscle tension, insomnia) and emotionally (anxiety, irritability, overwhelm). These are signs that your work is taking a toll on your health, and it's important to address them before they escalate.

Exercise: Creating Your Work-Life Balance Plan

Here are some practical exercises to help you create and maintain a healthy work-life balance:

1. **Design Your Ideal Work Schedule**:
   - Write down the number of hours you want to dedicate to work each week, and create a schedule that fits within those hours. Include specific time blocks for work tasks and personal activities, ensuring you have enough time for both.

2. **Set Non-Negotiable Boundaries**:

- o Identify two or three key boundaries that you want to enforce to protect your personal time. These could be things like "no work after 6 PM," "weekends are for family," or "no emails during dinner." Write them down and commit to following them.

3. **Schedule a Weekly Personal Activity**:
   - o Choose one personal activity that brings you joy and make it a non-negotiable part of your weekly routine. This could be a hobby, exercise, spending time with friends, or simply relaxing. Schedule it into your calendar, just like you would a work task.

4. **Track Your Energy Levels**:
   - o For one week, track your energy levels at different points in the day. Note when you feel most productive and when you feel drained. Use this information to optimize your schedule, focusing on important tasks during your peak energy times and taking breaks when needed.

Conclusion: The Balance of Success

True success isn't just about achieving your goals—it's about doing so in a way that's sustainable and fulfilling. By maintaining a healthy work-life balance, you protect your well-being, sustain your passion, and enjoy the journey, not just the destination. Remember, a balanced life leads to greater creativity, productivity, and long-term happiness, both in your work and personal life.

In the next chapter, we'll explore how to create long-term strategies for scaling your venture and achieving your bigger goals, while maintaining the balance and well-being you've worked hard to establish.

Chapter 10: Scaling Your Venture—Expanding Without Losing Focus

"Scaling your venture isn't just about growing bigger—it's about growing smarter, maintaining quality, and staying true to your vision."

After establishing a solid foundation and achieving initial success with your venture, the next challenge is scaling. Scaling your venture means expanding your reach, increasing your capacity, and generating more revenue without losing the core values that made your venture successful in the first place.

Scaling can be exciting, but it also requires careful planning, smart resource allocation, and a focus on sustainability. This chapter will guide you through the process of scaling your venture while maintaining focus, quality, and balance.

What Does It Mean to Scale a Venture?

Scaling is different from simply growing. While growth often involves adding more resources (more staff, more products, more customers), scaling focuses on increasing efficiency and capacity without proportionally increasing costs or complexity. In other words, scaling means doing more with what you already have, or making smart investments that yield higher returns.

Here's what scaling might look like for your venture:

1. **Increased Capacity**:
   o Scaling allows you to handle more customers, clients, or products without overwhelming your current resources. It could mean automating processes, optimizing workflows, or expanding your team.
2. **Expanding Your Reach**:
   o As you scale, you may reach new markets, expand geographically, or target different customer segments. This could involve launching new products, entering new industries, or using marketing to attract a larger audience.
3. **Improving Efficiency**:
   o Scaling often involves finding ways to improve efficiency, allowing you to produce more with fewer resources. This might include automating tasks, streamlining operations, or optimizing supply chains.
4. **Growing Revenue**:
   o Ultimately, scaling aims to increase revenue without significantly increasing costs. The goal is to maximize profitability by using your resources wisely and strategically.

Step 1: Assessing Readiness to Scale

Before diving into the process of scaling, it's important to assess whether your venture is ready. Scaling too early or too fast can lead to issues with quality, customer service, or financial strain. Here are some key indicators that you're ready to scale:

1. **Consistent Demand**:
   o If you've seen consistent demand for your products or services over a period of time, this is a good sign that your venture can handle growth. Ensure that your demand is not based on temporary trends but reflects ongoing customer interest.

   Example: If your online store has been steadily increasing sales for six months, it might be time to scale up your inventory or expand into new product categories.

2. **Strong Financial Health**:
   o Before scaling, make sure your finances are in order. You should have a positive cash flow, healthy profit margins, and enough capital to invest in growth. Scaling often requires an initial investment, so ensure you're financially prepared.

   Example: Review your profit margins and ensure that you have a clear plan for covering the costs of scaling, such as additional staff, marketing, or new technology.

3. **Solid Systems and Processes**:
   o Scaling requires robust systems that can handle increased demand. Review your current processes to ensure they are

efficient and scalable. Weak processes will only become more problematic as you grow.

Example: If you're managing orders manually and it's becoming overwhelming, consider investing in an automated order management system before scaling further.

4. **Clear Vision for Growth**:
   o Scaling should align with your long-term vision. Do you want to expand your product line, enter new markets, or increase sales in your existing market? Having a clear growth strategy helps ensure that you scale in the right direction.

Example: Decide whether your goal is to grow vertically (offering more services to existing customers) or horizontally (expanding into new markets or customer segments).

Step 2: Scaling Smartly—Key Strategies

Once you've determined that your venture is ready to scale, it's time to create a plan. Scaling isn't about doing everything at once—it's about focusing on strategic areas that yield the highest returns. Here are some smart strategies for scaling your venture:

1. **Automate Where Possible**:
   o One of the most effective ways to scale is by automating repetitive tasks.

Automation frees up your time and resources, allowing you to focus on high-impact activities. From marketing to customer service, automation can streamline many areas of your venture.

Example: Use email marketing automation to send personalized emails to customers based on their purchase history, freeing up time for other marketing efforts.

2. **Outsource Non-Core Tasks**:
   o As you scale, consider outsourcing tasks that aren't central to your venture's success. Outsourcing allows you to focus on your core competencies while letting experts handle specialized or time-consuming tasks.

Example: Outsource bookkeeping, website maintenance, or graphic design to freelancers, allowing you to focus on product development and customer relations.

3. **Leverage Technology**:
   o Investing in the right technology can significantly enhance your ability to scale. From project management tools to customer relationship management (CRM) systems, technology can help you manage more clients, process more orders, and communicate more effectively.

Example: Implement a project management tool to keep track of tasks, deadlines, and team collaboration, allowing you to handle more projects without sacrificing quality.

4. **Focus on Customer Retention**:
    o Acquiring new customers is important, but retaining existing ones is often more cost-effective. Loyal customers not only provide repeat business but can also become advocates for your brand. Focus on building strong relationships with your customers through excellent service and personalized experiences.

    Example: Implement a loyalty program that rewards repeat customers with discounts, special offers, or early access to new products.

5. **Expand Your Offerings**:
    o Scaling doesn't always mean acquiring more customers—it can also mean increasing your revenue from existing customers. Consider adding complementary products or services that align with what your customers already love.

    Example: If you sell handmade jewellery, consider offering personalized engraving or gift packaging as an additional service.

Step 3: Managing the Challenges of Scaling

Scaling brings opportunities, but it also introduces new challenges. As your venture grows, it's important to manage these challenges effectively to maintain quality and avoid burnout. Here's how to navigate the common challenges of scaling:

1. **Maintaining Quality**:
   - As you scale, maintaining the quality of your products or services is crucial. Growth shouldn't come at the expense of the customer experience. Keep quality control systems in place and don't compromise on your standards.

   Example: If you're producing more products, invest in better materials or hire additional team members to ensure that each product meets your standards.

2. **Managing Increased Demand**:
   - As your venture grows, you'll need to manage increased demand without overwhelming yourself or your team. Consider hiring additional staff, outsourcing certain tasks, or investing in technology to handle larger volumes.

   Example: If you're receiving more orders than you can handle, hire part-time help during peak periods or partner with a fulfillment centre to manage shipping.

3. **Protecting Your Vision and Values**:
   - Growth can sometimes lead to losing sight of your original vision or values. Stay true to the mission that drove you to start your venture in the first place. Make sure that every decision you make

aligns with your long-term goals and principles.

Example: If sustainability is a core value of your venture, make sure that as you scale, your practices remain eco-friendly, even if it means sourcing materials from new suppliers.

4. **Handling Cash Flow**:
   o Scaling often requires upfront investments, which can strain your cash flow. Make sure to carefully plan your finances and avoid overextending yourself. Create a realistic budget for scaling, and explore funding options if needed.

   Example: If you need capital to scale, consider a small business loan, crowdfunding, or bringing in investors who align with your values.

Step 4: Long-Term Growth and Sustainability

Scaling isn't just about short-term success—it's about setting your venture up for long-term growth and sustainability. Here's how to ensure that your venture continues to thrive as it scales:

1. **Measure Key Metrics**:
   o As you scale, track key performance metrics such as revenue growth,

customer acquisition cost, profit margins, and customer retention rates. These metrics give insight into how well your venture is scaling and where you can improve.

Example: Track customer satisfaction rates by sending out surveys after purchases. Use this feedback to continually improve your customer experience.

2. **Reinvest in Growth**:
   o Once you start seeing returns from scaling, reinvest a portion of your profits back into the venture. This could be in the form of new product development, hiring additional staff, or improving your marketing efforts.

Example: If your business is thriving, reinvest in expanding your product line or entering a new market to continue growing.

3. **Stay Adaptable**:
   o The market will continue to evolve, so stay adaptable and ready to pivot if needed. Keep an eye on industry trends, customer preferences, and technological advancements that could impact your venture.

Example: If new technologies emerge that could make your business more efficient or competitive, be open to adopting them and adjusting your processes.

Exercise: Scaling Your Venture

Let's put some of these strategies into action! Here are exercises to help you start scaling your venture:

1. **Identify Key Areas for Automation**:
   - Review your current operations and identify repetitive tasks that could be automated. Research tools or software that could help streamline these tasks, freeing up time for more important work.
2. **Create a Customer Retention Strategy**:
   - Develop a plan to retain existing customers. This could include loyalty programs, personalized offers, follow-up emails, or exceptional customer service strategies. Think about how you can keep your customers engaged and encourage repeat business.

3. **Assess Your Financial Readiness**:
   - Review your current financial situation and determine if you're financially ready to scale. Create a detailed budget for scaling, including any upfront investments you'll need to make (e.g., hiring, marketing, technology) and how you plan to cover these costs.
4. **Outline a New Offering**:
   - Think about an additional product or service you could offer to your existing customers. What would complement your current offerings? Write down the

steps needed to develop and launch this new offering, and consider how it fits into your overall growth strategy.

5. **Track Key Metrics**:
   - Identify the key metrics you'll use to measure the success of your scaling efforts. These could include customer acquisition costs, profit margins, customer satisfaction, and revenue growth. Set up a system for tracking these metrics over time to evaluate your progress.

Conclusion: Scaling with Purpose and Precision

Scaling your venture is an exciting step, but it requires careful planning, smart investments, and a focus on sustainability. By automating tasks, outsourcing when necessary, and focusing on customer retention, you can grow your venture without sacrificing quality or your original vision. Remember, scaling isn't about rapid expansion—it's about thoughtful, strategic growth that aligns with your long-term goals. In the next chapter, we'll explore how to build a strong brand that resonates with your audience, reflects your values, and sets you apart from competitors as you continue to grow.

Chapter 11: Building a Strong Brand—Creating a Lasting Impression

"Your brand is more than just a logo or a name—it's the story you tell, the values you represent, and the connection you create with your audience."

As your venture grows, one of the most important assets you can develop is your brand. A strong brand isn't just about standing out in a crowded market—it's about building a connection with your audience, conveying your mission and values, and creating a lasting impression that resonates with people on a deeper level.

In this chapter, we'll explore how to define your brand's identity, craft a compelling brand story, and create consistency across all platforms. Building a strong brand helps foster customer loyalty, differentiate you from competitors, and give your venture a unique voice and presence.

Why Your Brand Matters

Your brand is how your audience perceives you, and it's much more than just your business name or logo. It's the sum total of your values, messaging, visuals, and the experiences you provide. A strong brand offers several key advantages:

1. **Differentiation**:

- o A well-defined brand sets you apart from competitors by highlighting what makes you unique. In a crowded marketplace, differentiation is key to standing out and being memorable.

2. **Customer Loyalty**:
   - o A strong brand builds trust and emotional connections with your audience. Customers who resonate with your brand are more likely to become loyal supporters, making repeat purchases and recommending you to others.

3. **Clear Communication**:
   - o Your brand communicates who you are, what you do, and why it matters. A consistent and clear brand message helps your audience understand your mission, values, and the benefits of your products or services.

4. **Recognition**:
   - o Consistent branding creates recognition. The more recognizable your brand, the easier it is for customers to find you and remember you when they need your product or service.

Step 1: Defining Your Brand Identity

Your brand identity is the essence of who you are and what your venture stands for. It includes your mission, values, personality, and the visual elements that represent your brand. Defining your brand identity is the first step toward creating a lasting impression.

1. **Clarify Your Mission**:
   - Your mission is the purpose behind your venture. Why did you start your business? What problem are you solving, and what impact do you want to have on your customers or the world? A clear mission gives your brand direction and purpose.

   Example: If you started a sustainable clothing line, your mission might be to provide high-quality fashion while reducing environmental impact. This mission should be central to your brand messaging and decision-making.

2. **Identify Your Core Values**:
   - Your values are the principles that guide your decisions and how you interact with customers. Are you focused on sustainability, innovation, transparency, or community? Defining your core values helps you build a brand that aligns with what your audience cares about.

   Example: If one of your core values is quality, it should be reflected in everything from your product materials to customer service. Make sure your values are visible in both your actions and messaging.

3. **Define Your Brand Personality**:
   - Just like a person, your brand has a personality. Is your brand fun and playful, or serious and professional? Is it approachable or exclusive? Your brand's

personality should resonate with your target audience and be consistent across all touchpoints.

Example: If your audience is young and creative, a playful and modern brand personality might resonate more than a formal or corporate tone. Let your brand's personality shine through in your messaging, visuals, and customer interactions.

4. **Create a Visual Identity**:
   - Your visual identity includes your logo, color palette, typography, and imagery. These elements should reflect your brand's personality and be consistent across all platforms. A strong visual identity helps create recognition and professionalism.

Example: Choose a colour palette that aligns with your brand's values and tone. If you run a health and wellness brand, calming colours like green and blue might work well. Make sure your logo and visuals are simple, memorable, and consistent.

Step 2: Crafting Your Brand Story

Your brand story is the narrative that explains who you are, what you do, and why it matters. A compelling brand story helps create emotional connections with your audience and gives your brand a human touch. Here's how to craft a powerful brand story:

1. **Start with Your Origin**:
   - Every brand has a story about how it began. Why did you start your venture? What inspired you? Sharing your origin story helps your audience relate to you on a personal level and understand the passion behind your work.

   Example: If you started your business out of frustration with the lack of eco-friendly products, sharing that personal journey adds authenticity to your brand.

2. **Highlight the Problem You're Solving**:
   - Great brands address a specific problem or need. What challenges are your customers facing, and how does your venture provide a solution? Be clear about the problem you solve and why it matters to your audience.

   Example: If your venture provides affordable tutoring services, your brand story could highlight the challenges students face in accessing quality education and how your service fills that gap.

3. **Share Your Mission and Vision**:
   - Your mission is what drives you, and your vision is what you aim to achieve in the future. Sharing both helps your audience understand your long-term goals and the impact you want to have. This creates a sense of purpose that resonates with people who share similar values.

Example: If your brand is focused on empowering women entrepreneurs, your vision might be to create a global network of female-led businesses that support and uplift one another.

4. **Be Authentic and Transparent**:
   - Authenticity is key to building trust. Share the ups and downs of your journey, the challenges you've faced, and how you've overcome them. Transparency makes your brand more relatable and human, allowing people to connect with your story.

Example: If your business went through a difficult time during the early stages, sharing that experience can create a deeper connection with your audience. People appreciate honesty and resilience.

Step 3: Building Consistency Across Platforms

Consistency is one of the most important aspects of building a strong brand. Your audience should have the same experience with your brand whether they're visiting your website, following you on social media, or purchasing your product. Here's how to ensure consistency:

1. **Use the Same Visuals**:

o Your logo, color palette, and fonts should be consistent across all platforms, from your website to social media to packaging. This helps reinforce brand recognition and professionalism.

Example: If your website uses a specific font and colour scheme, make sure those elements are reflected in your business cards, social media posts, and advertisements.

2. **Maintain a Consistent Tone**:
   o Your brand's voice and tone should be the same across all forms of communication. Whether you're sending an email, writing a blog post, or interacting with customers on social media, your tone should reflect your brand's personality and values.

Example: If your brand is light-hearted and casual, keep that tone in your email newsletters and social media responses. Consistency in tone builds familiarity and trust with your audience.

3. **Align Your Messaging**:
   o Your core message—what your brand stands for and the value you provide—should be consistent across all channels. Whether it's a tagline, mission statement, or product description, make sure your messaging aligns with your overall brand identity.

Example: If your brand's message is about sustainability, make sure that message is clear on your website, social media, and packaging. Customers should always understand your brand's mission, no matter where they interact with you.

4. **Engage Consistently**:
   - Consistency also applies to how often you engage with your audience. Regular updates, posts, and interactions help build a relationship with your customers. Create a content calendar to ensure you're consistently sharing valuable information and staying top of mind.

   Example: Plan a social media schedule where you post regularly—whether it's daily, weekly, or biweekly. Consistency builds trust and keeps your audience engaged.

Step 4: Evolving Your Brand Over Time

A strong brand doesn't stay static—it evolves over time as your business grows and the market changes. While consistency is important, it's equally important to stay flexible and adapt to new trends or customer preferences.

1. **Listen to Customer Feedback**:
   - Pay attention to what your customers are saying about your brand. Use feedback to refine your messaging, improve your offerings, or adjust your brand's visual identity. Listening to your audience helps keep your brand relevant.

Example: If customers consistently ask for more eco-friendly packaging, consider evolving your brand to reflect a stronger commitment to sustainability.

2. **Stay Current with Industry Trends**:
   o Keep an eye on industry trends and market shifts that might impact your brand. Staying updated allows you to innovate and adapt, ensuring your brand remains competitive and aligned with customer expectations.

Example: If you're in the tech industry, adopting new technologies or trends, such as AI or automation, can position your brand as forward-thinking and innovative.

3. **Revisit Your Mission and Values**:
   o As your venture grows, periodically revisit your mission and values to ensure they still align with your goals and audience. While your core mission may stay the same, the way you communicate or embody those values may evolve.

Example: If you started your business as a local venture and have now expanded internationally, your brand message might shift to reflect a broader, more global perspective.

4. **Keep Your Brand Story Alive**:

- As your venture evolves, keep your brand story alive by sharing updates, milestones, and new chapters of your journey. Let your audience in on the behind-the-scenes moments, challenges, and successes that shape your brand's growth. This keeps your brand story dynamic and relatable.

Example: If your business reaches a significant milestone, such as expanding to new markets or launching a new product line, share that part of your journey with your audience. Let them celebrate with you and feel like they're part of your ongoing success story.

Exercise: Building and Strengthening Your Brand

Now that you have a clearer understanding of the key elements of a strong brand, here are a few exercises to help you define and strengthen your brand identity:

1. **Create a Brand Identity Worksheet**:
   - Write down your mission, core values, and brand personality. Describe how you want your brand to be perceived by your audience. Then, define your visual identity, including colors, fonts, and imagery that align with your brand's personality.
2. **Write Your Brand Story**:
   - Develop a compelling narrative that explains how your venture started, the problem it solves, and the mission that drives you forward. Share the emotional

journey behind your brand and why it matters to your audience.

3. **Conduct a Brand Audit**:
   o Review your current branding across all platforms—website, social media, packaging, emails, etc.—and assess whether everything is consistent. Is your message clear and aligned with your brand values? Are your visuals cohesive? Make adjustments as needed to ensure consistency.

4. **Engage with Your Audience**:
   o Start a conversation with your customers or followers. Ask them what they love about your brand, what they'd like to see more of, and what makes them loyal to your products or services. Use their feedback to refine your brand and strengthen your connection with them.

5. **Update Your Brand Guidelines**:
   o Create or update your brand guidelines—a document that outlines your brand's mission, values, voice, tone, and visual elements. These guidelines will help maintain consistency as your brand grows and expands across platforms.

Conclusion: The Power of a Strong Brand

A strong brand is one of the most valuable assets your venture can have. It's the key to building lasting relationships with your audience, differentiating yourself from competitors, and creating a memorable and impactful presence in the market.

By defining your brand identity, crafting a compelling story, and maintaining consistency across all touchpoints, you create a brand that resonates deeply with your customers.

In the next chapter, we'll explore how to leverage your brand's success to build partnerships, collaborations, and lasting relationships with others in your industry—taking your venture to the next level.

Chapter 12: Building Strategic Partnerships and Collaborations

"Success in business is not just about what you know, but who you work with. Strategic partnerships can unlock new opportunities and drive growth beyond your own capabilities."

As your venture grows, collaborating with others in your industry can open doors to new markets, expand your reach, and provide valuable resources you might not have on your own. Whether through partnerships, alliances, or collaborations, building strategic relationships allows you to scale your business more effectively, increase brand visibility, and leverage the strengths of others to drive mutual success.

In this chapter, we'll explore how to identify the right partners, foster mutually beneficial collaborations, and create lasting relationships that contribute to the long-term growth of your venture.

Why Partnerships and Collaborations Matter

Strategic partnerships and collaborations are a powerful way to grow your venture without having to take on all the work yourself. These relationships can help you:

1. **Access New Markets**:
   - Partnering with others can give you access to new customer bases or geographic regions that you wouldn't otherwise reach on your own. This can be particularly useful when expanding your business into unfamiliar territories.
2. **Leverage Complementary Skills**:
   - Collaborating with a partner who has strengths that complement your own allows both of you to offer more value to your customers. For example, if you're a product-based business, partnering with a service provider can enhance your offering.
3. **Share Resources and Expertise**:
   - Partnerships can provide access to resources such as distribution channels, technology, or specialized knowledge that might otherwise be expensive or difficult to obtain. Sharing expertise can lead to improved products, services, or operational efficiencies.
4. **Increase Brand Visibility**:
   - Collaborating with well-known brands or influencers in your industry can boost your brand's visibility and credibility. This increased exposure can lead to new customers, more followers, and greater awareness of your venture.
5. **Reduce Costs and Risks**:
   - By sharing resources or entering joint ventures, you can reduce operational costs or mitigate risks associated with expansion. Partners often share the

financial burden of new initiatives, making growth more feasible.

Step 1: Identifying the Right Partners

Not every potential partnership is a good fit for your business. Successful collaborations come from finding partners whose values, goals, and strengths align with your own. Here's how to identify the right partners for your venture:

1. **Shared Values and Vision**:
   - The best partnerships are built on shared values and a common vision. Look for partners whose mission aligns with yours, and who are motivated by similar goals. This ensures that you both have the same priorities and work towards a mutually beneficial outcome.

   Example: If your venture focuses on sustainability, you'll want to collaborate with other businesses or organizations that share your commitment to eco-friendly practices. This alignment reinforces your brand's values and makes the partnership more authentic.

2. **Complementary Strengths**:
   - A good partnership involves two parties bringing different but complementary strengths to the table. Look for partners whose expertise or resources complement your own. This creates a

win-win scenario where both parties benefit from the collaboration.

Example: If you specialize in product design but struggle with marketing, partnering with a company that excels in marketing and branding can help both ventures grow together.

3. **Aligned Target Audience**:
   o Consider whether your partner's audience overlaps with or complements your own. Successful collaborations allow both partners to access new customer bases without cannibalizing each other's markets. Ensure that the partnership introduces your venture to an audience that would naturally be interested in your products or services.

Example: A fitness brand might collaborate with a health-focused meal service, allowing both to reach customers interested in wellness while offering them a holistic solution.

4. **Reputation and Trustworthiness**:
   o The reputation of your partners can affect how your brand is perceived. It's important to choose partners who have a strong track record and are trusted by their customers or industry peers. Doing due diligence on potential partners can protect your brand from being associated with unethical or unreliable companies.

Example: Before partnering with another company, research their reputation online, review customer feedback, and consider whether their approach to customer service and quality aligns with yours.

Step 2: Building Mutually Beneficial Collaborations

Once you've identified a potential partner, the next step is creating a collaboration that benefits both parties. A successful partnership should be fair, transparent, and centred on achieving shared goals. Here's how to create strong, mutually beneficial collaborations:

1. **Set Clear Goals and Expectations**:
   - Begin by outlining the specific goals of the collaboration. What do you want to achieve? What does success look like for both parties? Clearly define the responsibilities of each partner, timelines, and how you'll measure results. This helps avoid misunderstandings and ensures that both parties are aligned from the start.

   Example: If you're launching a joint product with a partner, decide who will handle product development, marketing, and distribution. Agree on how profits will be shared and how success will be evaluated.

2. **Leverage Each Partner's Strengths**:
   - Make sure the collaboration is structured in a way that plays to each partner's

strengths. By allowing each partner to focus on what they do best, you maximize the effectiveness of the partnership and improve the chances of achieving shared goals.

Example: In a collaboration between a graphic designer and a printer, the designer might focus on creating the visuals, while the printer handles production and distribution. Both parties contribute their expertise to the project.

3. **Communicate Openly and Regularly**:
   o Clear and consistent communication is essential for the success of any partnership. Schedule regular check-ins to discuss progress, address challenges, and make adjustments as needed. Open communication ensures that both parties stay on the same page and can respond quickly to any changes or issues.

Example: Set up a weekly or biweekly meeting with your partner to review key performance indicators (KPIs), share updates, and discuss any changes in strategy.

4. **Create a Win-Win Agreement**:
   o The best partnerships are those where both parties feel they are benefiting equally. Ensure that the terms of the partnership are fair, with both sides gaining something valuable—whether it's revenue, exposure, expertise, or resources.

Example: If you're co-hosting an event with a partner, ensure both brands receive equal billing in the marketing materials, and share the workload equally to maximize the event's success.

Step 3: Expanding Through Strategic Partnerships

As your venture grows, strategic partnerships can play a critical role in scaling your business and reaching new heights. Here are ways to use partnerships to expand your reach and influence:

1. **Cross-Promote with Like-Minded Brands**:
   - Partnering with complementary brands for cross-promotion is a cost-effective way to expand your reach. By promoting each other's products or services, you both gain access to new customers without the expense of paid advertising.

   Example: A skincare company might collaborate with a wellness influencer to cross-promote products on social media. The influencer gains high-quality products to showcase, while the skincare company reaches the influencer's audience.

2. **Co-Create New Products or Services**:
   - Co-creating a product or service with a partner can lead to innovative offerings that attract new customers and increase

revenue. Collaborative products can generate buzz and offer a fresh perspective to both brands' audiences.

Example: A coffee company and a local bakery could create a signature coffee blend and pastry pairing, offering it as a special promotion that appeals to both their customer bases.

3. **Host Joint Events or Webinars**:
   o Hosting events or webinars with a partner can boost brand visibility, attract new customers, and position both brands as leaders in their respective fields. Events allow you to engage directly with your audience and provide value through education, networking, or entertainment.

Example: A tech start-up might collaborate with a software company to host a webinar on improving workplace productivity using digital tools. Both companies benefit from the exposure and thought leadership.

4. **Tap into International Markets**:
   o If you're looking to expand internationally, partnering with businesses in your target markets can help you navigate cultural differences, regulations, and local consumer behavior. A local partner can provide the expertise and connections needed to enter new regions smoothly.

Example: A fashion brand might partner with a well-established retail chain in another country to distribute its products, helping it gain credibility and reach a wider audience without setting up its own operations abroad.

Step 4: Nurturing Long-Term Relationships

Successful collaborations are often built on long-term relationships. Rather than seeing partnerships as one-time deals, focus on building lasting connections that can evolve and grow over time. Here's how to nurture long-term relationships:

1. **Deliver on Your Promises**:
   - Always follow through on your commitments. Delivering high-quality work and meeting deadlines builds trust and credibility, encouraging partners to continue working with you in the future.

   Example: If you've agreed to provide promotional materials by a certain date, make sure they're delivered on time and exceed expectations. Consistency fosters confidence in your ability to collaborate effectively.

2. **Show Appreciation**:
   - Recognize and celebrate the success of your partnerships. Whether through public shout-outs, thank-you notes, or special offers, showing appreciation reinforces the relationship and encourages future collaborations.

Example: After a successful joint event or product launch, send a personalized note of thanks to your partner and celebrate the results together.

3. **Be Open to Feedback and Improvement**:
   - Collaboration often involves learning from each other. Be open to feedback from your partners and use it as an opportunity to improve future collaborations. Likewise, offer constructive feedback to help your partners grow as well.

Example: After completing a joint project, ask your partner for feedback on how the collaboration went and what could be improved for future partnerships. Use this feedback to refine your approach and strengthen the relationship.

4. **Explore New Opportunities Together**:
   - As your partnership evolves, look for new opportunities to collaborate. This could include launching new products, entering new markets, or working together on larger-scale projects. Long-term partners can become valuable allies in driving mutual growth and success.

Example: If you've collaborated successfully on a small project, explore the possibility of expanding the partnership to include new product lines, joint marketing campaigns, or even co-branded events.

Exercise: Finding and Building Partnerships

Here are a few practical exercises to help you identify potential partners and build strategic collaborations:

1. **Identify 3 Potential Partners**:
   - Make a list of three potential partners in your industry or related fields. Research their values, audience, and strengths to determine if they align with your venture. Reach out to them with a proposal for collaboration that benefits both parties.
2. **Draft a Partnership Proposal**:
   - Write a draft partnership proposal outlining the specific goals, responsibilities, and benefits of the collaboration. Focus on how both parties will benefit and what you bring to the table. Having a clear proposal helps get the conversation started on the right foot.
3. **Analyse a Competitor's Partnerships**:
   - Look at successful partnerships or collaborations that your competitors or industry leaders have formed. What made them successful? How can you apply similar strategies to your own venture?
4. **Develop a Co-Promotion Strategy**:
   - Think of a like-minded brand or influencer you could collaborate with for cross-promotion. Develop a plan for how you could promote each other's products or services, whether through social

media, email campaigns, or shared content.

5. **Track the Success of Your Collaborations**:
   - Once you've formed a partnership, track key metrics such as sales, customer engagement, and brand visibility to measure the success of the collaboration. Use this data to evaluate whether the partnership should be continued or expanded.

Conclusion: The Power of Collaboration

Strategic partnerships and collaborations are powerful tools for expanding your venture, gaining access to new markets, and leveraging the strengths of others to grow more effectively.

By identifying the right partners, creating mutually beneficial collaborations, and nurturing long-term relationships, you open the door to new opportunities that can take your venture to the next level.

In the next chapter, we'll explore how to evaluate your venture's impact, measure success, and adjust your strategy for continuous improvement and long-term sustainability.

Chapter 13: Measuring Success and Continuous Improvement—Refining Your Strategy for Long-Term Growth

---

"Success isn't a one-time event—it's a continuous process of evaluation, learning, and improvement."

No matter how successful your venture becomes, the journey doesn't stop. To maintain and grow that success, it's important to regularly evaluate your performance, learn from your experiences, and make strategic adjustments along the way. This process of measuring success and seeking continuous improvement helps you stay on track, respond to changes in the market, and ensure your venture's long-term sustainability.

In this chapter, we'll explore how to define success for your venture, the key metrics you should be tracking, and how to use data and feedback to refine your strategy over time. Continuous improvement is not just about fixing what's broken—it's about finding ways to be even better, more efficient, and more effective.

Why Measuring Success Matters

Measuring success goes beyond looking at profits or sales numbers. It's about evaluating the overall health of your venture, understanding what's working and what isn't, and identifying areas for growth and improvement. Here's why measuring success is critical:

1. **Identify Strengths and Weaknesses**:
   o Regularly assessing your venture's performance helps you understand where you're excelling and where you may need to improve. This allows you to build on your strengths and address weaknesses before they become major issues.
2. **Make Data-Driven Decisions**:
   o Tracking key metrics allows you to make informed, data-driven decisions. Instead of relying on gut feelings, you can use real data to guide your strategy and ensure that your choices are aligned with your goals.
3. **Ensure Long-Term Sustainability**:
   o Evaluating success isn't just about the short-term—it's about ensuring that your venture is on a path to long-term sustainability. By regularly reviewing your performance, you can make adjustments that help you adapt to market changes and stay relevant over time.
4. **Celebrate Milestones and Progress**:
   o Measuring success allows you to recognize and celebrate your progress. Achieving milestones, no matter how small, boosts motivation and keeps you and your team focused on the bigger picture.

Step 1: Defining Success for Your Venture

Success looks different for every venture. While financial goals are important, there are other ways to measure success, such as customer satisfaction, brand recognition, or personal fulfillment. Defining success for your venture is the first step toward measuring and improving it.

1. **Financial Success**:
   o Revenue, profit margins, and cash flow are the most obvious measures of financial success. However, success isn't just about making money—it's about profitability, managing costs, and ensuring that your venture remains financially healthy over time.

   Example: Set specific financial goals for revenue growth, profit margins, or reducing operational costs. These goals should be realistic and aligned with your long-term vision.

2. **Customer Satisfaction and Retention**:
   o Your customers are at the heart of your venture's success. High levels of customer satisfaction and retention are strong indicators of a healthy business. Satisfied customers are more likely to return and refer others, helping you grow organically.

   Example: Track customer reviews, feedback, and retention rates to measure how well your products or services are meeting customer needs. If you notice a decline in satisfaction, address the underlying issues to improve loyalty.

3. **Brand Recognition and Reputation**:
    o   A strong brand is essential for long-term success. Measuring your brand's recognition and reputation can help you understand how well your messaging resonates with your audience and how you're perceived in the market.

    Example: Track social media mentions, press coverage, and website traffic to evaluate your brand's visibility. Positive media coverage and customer reviews can indicate a strong brand reputation.

4. **Personal Fulfillment**:
    o   For many entrepreneurs, success isn't just about financial gains—it's about doing work that's meaningful and fulfilling. Personal fulfillment comes from pursuing your passion, making a positive impact, and achieving a sense of balance between work and life.

    Example: Regularly reflect on your personal goals and assess whether your venture aligns with them. Are you still passionate about the work you're doing? Are you maintaining a healthy work-life balance?

Step 2: Tracking Key Metrics

Once you've defined what success looks like for your venture, the next step is to track key performance metrics that provide insight into your progress. Here are some of the most important metrics to consider:

1. **Revenue and Profit Margins**:
   - Track your total revenue, gross profit margin, and net profit margin to ensure your venture is financially healthy. A growing revenue stream combined with stable or improving profit margins indicates that your business is scaling efficiently.

   Example: Use accounting software or spreadsheets to track monthly revenue and compare it against costs. Aim to increase your profit margins by reducing unnecessary expenses or optimizing pricing strategies.

2. **Customer Acquisition Cost (CAC)**:
   - Customer acquisition cost measures how much you spend to acquire a new customer. If your CAC is too high, it may indicate that marketing or sales strategies need adjustment. The goal is to lower CAC over time as you refine your marketing efforts.

   Example: Divide your total marketing and sales expenses by the number of new customers acquired during a specific period to calculate your CAC. Compare this with the lifetime value of a customer (LTV) to ensure you're spending efficiently.

3. **Customer Retention Rate**:
   - Retaining customers is often more cost-effective than acquiring new ones. A high customer retention rate indicates that your customers are satisfied and loyal. Track this metric to ensure that your venture is building long-term relationships with customers.

   Example: Calculate your retention rate by dividing the number of repeat customers by the total number of customers over a specific time period. Implement loyalty programs or personalized experiences to improve retention.

4. **Website Traffic and Conversion Rates**:
   - If your venture operates online, track website traffic, engagement, and conversion rates. Understanding how many visitors take action (such as making a purchase or signing up for a newsletter) helps you evaluate the effectiveness of your website and marketing campaigns.

   Example: Use tools like Google Analytics to track how many visitors come to your site, where they come from, and what actions they take. Optimize your website to improve conversion rates and turn visitors into customers.

5. **Social Media Engagement**:

- o Social media engagement metrics, such as likes, shares, comments, and follower growth, help you understand how well your content resonates with your audience. Strong engagement indicates that your brand is building relationships and gaining visibility.

Example: Track the performance of individual posts to see which content drives the most engagement. Use this data to refine your content strategy and post more of what your audience loves.

6. **Employee or Team Satisfaction**:
   - o If you have a team, their satisfaction and well-being play a major role in the success of your venture. Happy, motivated team members are more productive and invested in your venture's growth. Regularly check in with your team to gauge satisfaction and morale.

Example: Conduct anonymous employee satisfaction surveys or hold regular one-on-one meetings to discuss any concerns or ideas for improvement. Act on feedback to create a positive and supportive work environment.

Step 3: Using Feedback to Refine Your Strategy

Success isn't just about tracking numbers—it's about listening to feedback from customers, employees, and the market. Feedback provides valuable insights into areas that need improvement and helps you adjust your strategy in real time.

1. **Customer Feedback**:
   - Actively seek feedback from your customers through surveys, reviews, or direct conversations. Use their insights to improve your products, services, or customer experience. Pay attention to patterns in feedback, as they often point to areas that need attention.

   Example: After launching a new product, send out a customer satisfaction survey to gather feedback on the product's quality, usability, and value. Use the responses to refine the product or improve future launches.

2. **Employee or Team Feedback**:
   - Your team is on the front lines of your business, so their feedback can provide valuable insights into operational challenges, customer interactions, or internal processes. Encourage an open feedback culture where team members feel comfortable sharing their ideas and concerns.

Example: Hold regular team meetings or brainstorming sessions to gather input on how to improve workflows, address challenges, or make the work environment more supportive.

3. **Market Trends and Competitor Analysis**:
   o Stay informed about market trends and what your competitors are doing. This helps you identify opportunities for innovation or areas where your venture could improve. Being aware of industry developments allows you to adjust your strategy and stay competitive.

   Example: Regularly analyse competitors' products, marketing strategies, and customer reviews. Identify gaps or weaknesses in their offerings that you can address in your own business to differentiate yourself.

Step 4: Making Continuous Improvements

Once you've gathered data and feedback, the next step is to implement changes that drive continuous improvement. This process involves setting new goals, adjusting strategies, and refining your approach over time.

1. **Set Improvement Goals**:
   o Based on your evaluation, set specific goals for improvement. These could include increasing customer retention, lowering acquisition costs, improving product quality, or enhancing team

satisfaction. Make sure your goals are measurable and time-bound.

Example: If your customer retention rate is lower than desired, set a goal to increase it by 10% over the next six months by implementing a loyalty program or improving customer service.

2. **Experiment and Test**:
   o Don't be afraid to experiment with new ideas or strategies. Whether it's testing a new marketing campaign, launching a new product feature, or changing your pricing model, small tests can provide valuable insights into what works best for your venture.

**Example

Example: If you want to test a new pricing strategy, start with a small segment of your audience. Offer them a different pricing tier or bundled services and track how they respond. Use the results to decide whether to roll out the changes to your broader audience.

3. **Monitor and Adjust Regularly**:
   o Continuous improvement requires ongoing monitoring. Set regular intervals (monthly, quarterly, or annually) to review your key metrics, evaluate your progress, and adjust your strategy as needed. The business landscape can change quickly, so it's important to stay agile.

Example: Every quarter, review your revenue, customer feedback, and employee satisfaction data. Identify any areas where you didn't meet your goals and determine what adjustments you can make to improve results in the next quarter.

4. **Celebrate Successes and Learn from Failures**:
   o Celebrate the milestones and successes you achieve along the way, no matter how small. Recognizing progress boosts morale and keeps you motivated. Equally important, view failures as learning opportunities. Analyze what went wrong, learn from the experience, and make improvements.

Example: If a new product launch didn't meet expectations, review customer feedback, marketing effectiveness, and production quality to understand why. Use this insight to improve future product launches.

Step 5: Balancing Growth with Sustainability

While it's important to focus on growth and improvement, it's equally essential to ensure that your venture is sustainable in the long term. Rapid, unchecked growth can sometimes lead to burnout, cash flow issues, or quality problems. Balancing growth with sustainability ensures that your business remains healthy and successful over time.

1. **Scale Gradually**:
   - While ambitious growth plans are exciting, scaling too quickly can strain your resources and compromise the quality of your product or service. Take a measured approach to growth, ensuring you have the infrastructure and capacity to support it.

Example: Instead of expanding to a new market immediately, focus on optimizing your operations and solidifying your presence in your current market. This prepares you for smoother scaling when the time comes.

2. **Maintain a Healthy Cash Flow**:
   - Growth often requires investment, whether in new technology, marketing, or additional staff. Make sure you're maintaining a healthy cash flow to support these investments without overextending your financial resources.

Example: Use cash flow forecasting tools to predict future financial needs and adjust your expenses accordingly. Build an emergency fund to cover unexpected costs during periods of growth.

3. **Protect Your Core Values**:
   - As you grow, it's important to stay true to the core values that defined your venture from the beginning. Scaling should enhance your brand's mission and values, not dilute them. Customers are drawn to businesses with strong

values, and maintaining these values builds long-term loyalty.

Example: If your brand values sustainability, ensure that as you scale, your production methods remain eco-friendly, even if it means taking a slower path to growth.

4. **Balance Work and Personal Life**:
   o Continuous growth can sometimes lead to overwork and burnout. Protecting your personal well-being and maintaining a healthy work-life balance is essential for long-term success. Regularly reassess your priorities to ensure that you're balancing your personal and professional life effectively.

Example: Set boundaries between work and personal time, delegate tasks when necessary, and schedule regular breaks to prevent burnout. Remember that sustainable success is built on a healthy, energized leader.

Exercise: Evaluating and Improving Your Venture

Here are some practical exercises to help you implement continuous improvement strategies in your venture:

1. **Track Key Performance Metrics**:

- o Identify the most important metrics for your business (revenue, profit margins, customer retention, etc.) and create a system for tracking them regularly. Use spreadsheets or business analytics tools to monitor trends and evaluate your performance.

2. **Gather Customer Feedback**:
   - o Create a survey or feedback form for your customers to assess their satisfaction with your products or services. Use the insights you gather to identify areas where you can improve or enhance the customer experience.

3. **Conduct a SWOT Analysis**:
   - o Perform a SWOT (Strengths, Weaknesses, Opportunities, Threats) analysis of your business. Identify your current strengths and weaknesses, explore new opportunities, and recognize potential threats in the market. Use this analysis to refine your strategy.

4. **Set Improvement Goals**:
   - o Based on your evaluation, set three improvement goals for the next quarter. These could involve boosting customer satisfaction, improving efficiency, or increasing sales. Make sure the goals are specific, measurable, and tied to your long-term vision.

5. **Plan for Sustainable Growth**:
   - o Create a sustainable growth plan that balances ambitious goals with careful resource management. Focus on scaling in a way that preserves your venture's

core values, financial health, and long-term sustainability.

Conclusion: The Path to Long-Term Success

Success isn't a destination—it's an ongoing journey of continuous learning, evaluation, and improvement. By defining what success looks like for your venture, tracking key metrics, gathering feedback, and making thoughtful adjustments, you can ensure that your business not only grows but thrives in the long term. The process of continuous improvement keeps you agile, innovative, and prepared to meet the challenges and opportunities that lie ahead.

In the next chapter, we'll wrap up the key lessons from this book and explore how to apply what you've learned to your own venture, ensuring that you're equipped with the tools, strategies, and mindset to achieve lasting success.

Chapter 14: Bringing It All Together—Your Roadmap to Lasting Success

"Success is a journey, not a destination. It's built on passion, strategy, and the willingness to learn and grow every step of the way."

As we come to the final chapter of this book, it's time to reflect on everything you've learned and how you can apply these lessons to your own venture. Whether you're just starting out or already running a successful business, the key to long-term success lies in your ability to combine passion, strategy, and continuous improvement. By building a strong foundation, creating a powerful brand, nurturing relationships, and measuring success, you equip yourself with the tools to navigate the challenges and opportunities that come your way.

This chapter will help you bring everything together and provide a clear roadmap for moving forward with confidence and clarity.

The Key Lessons from This Book

Throughout this book, we've explored various aspects of building, growing, and sustaining a successful venture. Here's a summary of the key lessons that will guide you toward lasting success:

1. **Follow Your Passion with Purpose**:
   - Your passion is the foundation of your venture. But passion alone isn't enough—you need to channel it into a clear purpose that drives your business forward. Align your passion with the needs of your audience, and build a venture that solves problems or adds value to their lives.

   Key Takeaway: Passion with purpose leads to a venture that is not only fulfilling but also sustainable.

2. **Build a Strong Brand Identity**:
   - Your brand is the way your audience experiences your venture. It's more than just your logo or website—it's your values, your story, and the emotions you evoke in your customers. A strong brand identity sets you apart in the market and creates lasting connections with your audience.

   Key Takeaway: Build a brand that resonates with your audience by aligning your visuals, messaging, and values consistently.

3. **Understand and Engage Your Audience**:
   - Your audience is the heart of your business. To succeed, you must understand their needs, preferences, and pain points. Craft your products, services, and marketing strategies around them, and always seek ways to engage and build lasting relationships.

Key Takeaway: Know your audience well and always prioritize their needs in your decision-making.

4. **Create a Sustainable Financial Strategy**:
   - o Managing your finances wisely is crucial to sustaining and growing your venture. From budgeting to reinvestment, focus on strategies that increase your profit margins, improve cash flow, and ensure long-term financial health.

Key Takeaway: Success is not just about revenue—it's about profitability, financial discipline, and long-term sustainability.

5. **Embrace Continuous Learning and Adaptability**:
   - o The business world is constantly changing, and the most successful ventures are the ones that adapt. Stay curious, embrace new technologies and trends, and continuously seek opportunities to learn and grow.

Key Takeaway: Never stop learning. Adaptability is the key to staying relevant and competitive.

6. **Balance Growth with Well-Being**:
   - o Success shouldn't come at the cost of your well-being or work-life balance. Prioritize your mental, physical, and emotional health as you build your venture. Create a sustainable work-life

balance that allows you to stay energized and passionate about your work.

Key Takeaway: Balance is essential for long-term success. Take care of yourself so you can take care of your venture.

7. **Scale Smartly and Sustainably**:
   o Scaling your business is exciting, but it requires careful planning and execution. Focus on sustainable growth by leveraging partnerships, automating processes, and building a strong infrastructure. Avoid growing too quickly without the right support in place.

Key Takeaway: Scale thoughtfully. Growth should enhance your business, not overwhelm it.

8. **Measure Success and Improve Continuously**:
   o Success isn't a fixed point—it's an ongoing process of evaluation and improvement. Regularly measure your performance, track key metrics, and gather feedback. Use this data to refine your strategy and make continuous improvements.

Key Takeaway: Success is a journey of continuous growth. Regularly evaluate your progress and adapt as needed.

Your Roadmap to Lasting Success

To help you apply these lessons and move forward with confidence, here's a roadmap to guide you through the key stages of building, growing, and sustaining your venture:

1. **Start with a Clear Vision**:
   - Before you take any action, make sure you have a clear vision for what you want to achieve. Define your mission, values, and goals. Your vision will serve as your compass, guiding every decision you make.
2. **Build a Strong Foundation**:
   - Lay the groundwork for your venture by creating a solid business plan, defining your brand identity, and setting up efficient systems for managing your finances, operations, and customer relationships.
3. **Focus on Your Audience**:
   - Identify your target audience and build your products, services, and marketing strategies around their needs. Engage with your audience regularly through social media, emails, and personal interactions to build trust and loyalty.
4. **Create and Scale Thoughtfully**:
   - Once your foundation is in place, focus on growth. Scale your venture strategically by expanding your offerings, building partnerships, and leveraging technology. Always keep sustainability in mind and avoid growing too fast.

5. **Monitor, Measure, and Adapt**:
   - As your venture grows, continuously monitor your performance. Track key metrics such as revenue, customer satisfaction, and profit margins. Use data and feedback to refine your strategy and make improvements.
6. **Stay Balanced and Resilient**:
   - Remember to prioritize your well-being as you build your venture. Maintain a healthy work-life balance, and stay resilient in the face of challenges. Success is a long-term game, and your health and energy are essential for sustaining it.
7. **Celebrate Milestones and Keep Learning**:
   - Celebrate every success along the way, no matter how small. Recognize your achievements and use them as motivation to keep pushing forward. Never stop learning, growing, and adapting to new opportunities.

Conclusion: The Path to Your Success

You now have the knowledge, strategies, and tools to build and grow a venture that aligns with your passion, serves your audience, and achieves lasting success. The journey won't always be easy, but by staying focused, adaptable, and committed to continuous improvement, you can create a venture that not only thrives but also brings you fulfillment.

Remember, success isn't a destination—it's a process. Every step you take, every challenge you overcome, and every lesson you learn moves you closer to your goals. Stay true to your mission, surround yourself with supportive partners and customers, and always believe in your ability to succeed.

Here's to your continued growth, success, and fulfillment as you embark on the next stage of your entrepreneurial journey!